Newman's Mariology

Newman's Mariology

M. J. L. PERROTT

The Saint Austin Press
1997

THE SAINT AUSTIN PRESS
PO Box 610
Southampton
SO14 0YY

© 1997, M.J.L. Perrott
© 1997, This edition, The Saint Austin Press.

ISBN 1 901157 45 8

A catalogue record for this book is available from the British Library

Printed in Great Britain by BPC Wheatons, Exeter.

Dedicated to the Rosa Mystica

Contents

Introduction

Marian devotion has traditionally been one of the great areas of discord between the Catholic Church and the Churches of the Reformation. It is one of Newman's lesser known works, his *Meditations and Devotions*, compiled from an assortment of writings by a contemporary at the Birmingham Oratory, which reveals his extraordinary Marian piety. When this is compared with his Anglican writings on the Blessed Virgin, an enormous divergence becomes apparent between the Vicar of St Mary's and the Catholic Oratorian.

Newman's attitude to his reception into the Catholic Church on 9th October 1845 is more often more often than not understood as that of a Patristically minded Anglican, taking into a neo-scholastic Roman Church, the culture and ethos of Oxford High Anglicanism. This gives the impression that Newman's conversion was somehow hybrid, being the Newman of the Via Media clothed in an Oratorian habit. Such a view was reflected in some of the late Fr C S Dessain's commentaries, written at a time when ecumenical optimism was fervent, soon after Vatican II. Hence we find such comments as this about Newman's Anglican writings: "a classical, a truly catholic Catholicism."[1]

Newman's Anglican and Catholic Mariology respectively illustrate just how decisive was the conversion of 1845. Above all else it was the Catholic Church's Marian dogmas of the Bodily Assumption and the Immaculate Conception, coupled to popular Marian devotion, which delayed his reception. Indeed, the *Essay on Development* stands or falls on its central principle being able to

---

[1] CS Dessain, *Newman's Spiritual Themes*, p 17

account for this Catholic mariology as a development and not a distortion. The *Apologia* makes it quite clear that Newman went to Littlemore with these dogmas uppermost in his mind as preventing his conversion. Hence, if the Church of England was no longer Catholic, Rome was not Apostolic because of them. This is the reason for what may appear to be the inordinate delay in his conversion.

It is surprising then that Newman's mariology has been so overlooked. Recently two other short studies have been made but these do explore the question in any detail.[2] Such an omission has led to a one-sided view of Newman's spirituality. His Patristic and scriptural piety have been given a prominence disproportionate to that which he received upon becoming a Catholic. As will be seen, this included the rosary, Marian novena prayers, the Marian litanies including his own compositions in honour of the Immaculate Heart, the Salve Regina, the breviary office of Our Lady, the prayers for the Marian feasts in the general calendar, and the indulgenced prayers of the Raccolta. Most important of all, was the votive Mass of Our Lady to be found in the Roman Missal, in which the awesome power of Christ's sacrifice was pleaded through the intercession and mediation of Our Lady. These devotions divide Newman's Catholic prayer life markedly from his Anglican and with them indicate a theological development which is more than merely incidental.

With Newman's beatification now before the Congregation for the Causes of Saints, his mariology ought to be better known. It reveals a man, whose tender devotion towards the Mother of God, is comparable to the Church's greatest clients of Our Lady. The Newman whose love of 'Theotokos' was shared with the early Fathers, is the same Newman, who as Cardinal of the Holy

---

[2] L Govaert, *Our Lady in the Development of Newman's Sensus Fidelium and the Development of Marian Doctrine.* (Paper to the Washington Branch of the Ecumenical Society of the Blessed Virgin Mary.)

Roman Church, addressed her as 'Virgo Veneranda'. Such an exalted place in his devotional life, of she who caused him such difficulty in his Anglican period, also gives his *Meditations and Devotions*, an ecumenical significance. He was ever sensitive to the problems of non-Catholics with regard to Mary. His *Letter to Pusey* displays just such a sensitivity, arising out of Anglican inability to believe in the Immaculate Conception. Such forthright apologetic is much needed today where a fresh impetus in mariology would clarify Anglican thinking. Catholics, too, would benefit in helping those who are suffering from a misplaced ecumenism which wishes to see the traditional devotions replaced by a more 'healthy' Christocentric piety. To such Christians, Newman's Marian theology should help kindle their love of she whom Newman called the 'Mystical Rose'.

Chapter One

THE FATHERS OF THE CHURCH
AND DEVOTION TO MARY

Newman's conversion to the Catholic Church was largely due to patristic reading which he began in the summer vacation of 1828.[3] As the *Apologia* makes clear, it was the philosophical and mystical harmony of the Fathers which came like music to his inward ear.[4] The rationalism of the Oriel Common Room, dominated by Hawkins and Whately, had introduced the evangelical Newman to High Church ideas, but distinct from the worshipping life of the Catholic Church, these ideas were tending to draw out of Newman, not a genuine Catholicism, but an intellectual pride. He himself admitted:

> "The truth is, I was beginning to prefer intellectual excellence to moral."[5]

His patristic reading, begun in 1828, checked this nascent intellectual pride. The Fathers revealed to Newman something lacking in the High Church 'Catholicism' of the Oriel Common Room. They showed him how a rigorous theological method could be wedded to a mysticism which was neither anti-intellectual nor emotionally florid; in Newman's own words _ the Oriel Common Room "stank of logic".[6] In short, the Father's provided him with the perfect balance of intellectual precision and a spirituality both biblical and mystical:

---

[3] *Letters and Diaries* Vol XI Letter to W Banner, 8 November 1845.
[4] *Apologia* p 115 (Fontana Edition 1972)
[5] ibid p 105
[6] ibid p 226 In fact Newman was quoting an acquaintance.

> "I understand them to mean that the exterior world, physical and historical, was but the outward manifestation of realities greater than itself. Nature was a parable. Scripture was an allegory: pagan literature, philosophy, and mythology, properly understood, were but a preparation for the Gospel."[7]

Over the next seventeen years he was to immerse himself in the writings of the Fathers. From them his sacramental theology accrued, and to a lesser extent, his ecclesiology also. They were to lead to his distaste for the Reformers and for their liturgical revisions.[8]

It is important, then, to have some understanding of the nature of the Fathers' devotion to Our Lady if we are to appreciate just how radical was the change in Newman's devotion to her after 1845. His Catholic devotion was consistent with that of his beloved St Athanasius, in a way in which his Anglican was not.

We know that when he selected Hurrell Froude's breviary as a memento after the latter's death in 1836, Newman never intended to recite the direct invocation of Our Lady contained in it. Although it is only speculation, it is not unreasonable to assume that the Roman Breviary must have reinforced Newman's growing belief in the Protestant nature of the Anglican liturgy. In his private recitation we know from correspondence that he found its diversity and richness uplifting by comparison with Cranmer's truncated offices. All the more remarkable, then, was his persistent refusal to invoke Our Lady's intercession whilst an Anglican. This he regarded as inconsistent with the 39 Articles, as we shall see later. This important fact does raise a question mark

---

[7] ibid p 115
[8] Letter to J Williams 13 December 1838. Williams Deposit. Lambeth Dep 3/26.

over Newman's assimilation of the Father's doctrinal and mystical writings, whilst an Anglican. The Breviary office of Newman's day remained unchanged until the reforms under Pius X. In the office of Matins for the feasts of Our Lady, there are numerous extracts from the Fathers including St Irenaeus and St Ephrem the Syrian. The latter in particular must have struck Newman as extremely mariolatrous in his theology. Not only is Mary exalted incomparably higher than the angels, but she is given a role of mediatrix and intercessor which is identical with Catholic practice.

Nevertheless, it is now generally agreed that in his patristic reading Newman was blazing a trail for Anglicans. The Fathers had been approached by his predecessors very much through the filter of the Reformers. In practice this meant that Our Lady, whilst mentioned, was never given the prominence which such Fathers as St Ephrem or St Irenaeus gave to her in their devotional writings. Their eulogies on Our Lady's part in our redemption stem from the end of the third century and the end of the second century respectively. The following passages from St Ephrem, with their reference to Our Lady's Immaculate Conception, are nowhere to be found in Lancelot Andrewes or any other of the 17th century Anglican divines. They borrow heavily in their devotional manuals from the Orthodox Marian tradition, but always 'vetted', as it were, through Cranmer's liturgical tradition. Hence, St Ephrem's prayer would not be acceptable:

> "Thou and thy Mother are the only ones who
> are perfectly
> beautiful in every respect; for there is no spot in
> thee, O Lord, nor any taint in thy Mother."[9]

St Ephrem is even more explicit in this passage:

> "God's Eden is Mary; in her is no tree of

---

[9] St Ephrem *The Nisbis Hymn* 27. Quoted in P Palmer SJ *Mary in the Documents of the Church* p 23

knowledge (experience of good and evil), no serpent that harms, no Eve that kills; from her springs the tree of life that restores the exiles to Eden."[10]

The Anglican divines with whom Newman was most certainly familiar, as Tract 90 shows, viewed the Fathers retrospectively, looking backwards through the Reformation controversies. In particular, the popish doctrines and devotion concerning the Blessed Virgin Mary aroused the greatest hostility. For those in the Reformed tradition this devotion included a theology of merit which undermined justification by faith, a theology of an Immaculate Conception which undermined Mary's need for redemption, a theology of grace, which distorted the nature of sanctification, and worst of all, a theology of invocation which distorted Christ's all-sufficient atoning death. In this respect, Newman's approach to the Fathers was no different from the High Church Anglicans of the 17th century. Like them, he was governed by the 39 Articles of the Book of Common Prayer. This is certainly evident from his Anglican writings about Our Lady, where all these doctrines are avoided or alluded to with great circumspection. As we shall see, the Anglican Newman's *Blessed Virgin Mary* of the Book of Common Prayer is a more formal and ethereal woman than the tender and intimate *Our Lady* of Newman's Catholic devotions. This distinction is a question as much of spirituality as of theology and is not easy to delineate. But the question must be asked: 'what is peculiar to Newman's patristic devotion and method of understanding'?

In his own words, Newman himself has put his finger on his unique approach:
> "Whatever be the true way of interpreting the Fathers, and in particular the Apostolic Fathers, if a

---

[10] ibid p 22 *On the Annunciation of the Mother of God.* Hymn 3

> man begins by summoning them before him,
> instead of betaking himself to them, by seeking to
> make them evidence for modern dogmas, instead
> of throwing his mind upon the text, a drawing from
> their own doctrines, he will to a certainty miss their
> sense."[11]

T M Parker noted this distinction between Newman's approach to the Fathers and that of his Caroline predecessors, an approach which Keble and Pusey still adopted.[12]   Unlike his contemporary High Church Anglicans, who were more in the mould of the later non-jurors, Newman assimilated both the doctrine and the mysticism of the Fathers in a more systematic way. This led increasingly to a dissatisfaction with the Reformers, in particular with their liturgy, and constituted the great divide within the Tractarians.   This was tangibly represented by the subscription to the martyrs' memorial.   Pusey contributed, Newman did not.

There is an ambiguity running through Newman's understanding of the Fathers. On the one hand, he can appeal to them as his authority for the Anglican Via Media theology, a theology which he admits is less than perfect.   It is essentially theoretical and without precedent, so that in the end he concludes: "The present is an unsatisfactory, miserable state of things, yet I can grant no more."[13]   On the other, he insists that the Anglican view of authority is such that it allows the "Truth to be entirely objective and detached, not" (as the Roman) "lying hid in the

---

[11] *British Critic* January 1839 p 54

[12] T M Parker *The Rediscovery of the Fathers in 17th Century Anglicanism* in *The Rediscovery of Newman.* (His distinctive approach came as a surprise to Parker).

[13] *Apologia* p 179

bosom of the Church...."[14]   The implication throughout the *Via Media* is that whatever the weaknesses of the Anglican system, it does preserve better than the Roman, the Primitive Faith. He illustrates this point by a curious analogy. Rome is compared to a 'Madonna and Child', whilst Anglicanism to 'a calvary'. The former represents the Marian nature of Rome's Christology, with its supposed distortions and overpowering ecclesiastical authority. The calvary is the pure nakedness of Anglican faith with both the Church and Our Lady in the background. They are subservient to the Gospel, not obscuring it. It is clear by Newman's choice of these two illustrations, that the Marian question was the overwhelming question counting against Rome's Apostolicity. The ambiguity then lies in the apparent Mariology of the Fathers being more akin to Anglicanism than to Romanism, and yet in practice neither Rome nor the Orthodox disagreed in essentials. Hence, at the end of the *Prophetical Office* Newman seems to write in despair about his Via Media:

> "Now that our discussions draw to a close, the thought with which we entered on the subject, is apt to recur, when the excitement of the enquiry has subsided, and weariness has succeeded, that what has been said is a dream, the wanton exercise, rather than the practical conclusions of the intellect."[15]

It is Newman's attitude to the Marian devotions of the Fathers which perhaps shows up more clearly than anything else the selective nature of the Via Media's patristic basis.

At the heart of the patristic understanding of Our Lady's role in the economy of redemption was their understanding of the nature and person of her Son. It was a Christological question first.

---

[14] ibid p 180
[15] ibid p 182

Our Lady's prerogatives were thoroughly derivative; of herself she possessed nothing. This is beautifully expressed by a number of pre-Nicene Fathers. Paramount among their imagery is the analogy they make between Christ as the second Adam and Our Lady as the second Eve. Mary is associated in the work of redemption by virtue of her consent to the Incarnation of her Son. Whilst the use of Sacred Scripture is heavily allegorical and mystical, being pre-form critical, it is nevertheless consistent with the intention of the Scriptural writers. If, for example, St Paul can regard Our Lord as the second Adam, then it is not over-fanciful to suggest that Mary's consent is a recapitulation of Eve's disobedience. St Irenaeous has no qualms about such a comparison, allowing Our Lady to have a role in this process of recapitulation second only to her Son. Her consent, when viewed in this context, allows to her a mediatory role, which, although always derivative from her Son's mediation, does justice to her representative, maternal vocation. This theology stands in stark contrast to the Protestant view, which gives to Our Lady a merely passive, unrepresentative, individualistic significance. Newman had no difficulty with the first of these two understandings, although, as we shall see, he was unable to draw it to its logical conclusions, due largely due to the defects of the Anglican liturgy.

The Fathers, by contrast, in viewing Our Lady's consent as more than merely passive, could regard as meritorious her sanctity. This sanctity gave rise to a secondary mediation by virtue of her free-will and co-operation.

All this Newman read for the first time in the summer of 1828. We can illustrate something of what Newman must have read, by quoting two second-century authors. St Justin Martyr wring about 155 AD, sees Our Lady's consent as undoing the guile of the serpent's seduction of Eve. It is important to note that he specifically ascribes this to Christ alone, but also to Our Lady's consent freely given:

> "For Eve, an undefiled virgin, conceived the word of the serpent, and brought forth disobedience and death. But the Virgin Mary, filled with faith and joy ... gave birth to Him, concerning whom we have shown so many passages of Scripture were written."[16]

We find here the central theme of the patristic understanding of Mary. As the second Eve she assumes in inverse proportion to Eve's disobedience, the role of the representative human figure who, through obedience, is a co-mediator with her Son in man's redemption. The second Eve's imagery has implicit the whole of mariology: Mary's Divine Motherhood, her perpetual virginity, her mediation, her sinlessness, and the incorruptibility of her body. This parallel is clear when we remember that for the Fathers, Eve was immaculate before the Fall. She enjoyed perfect dialogue with God, was mother of the human race, and, according to tradition, would not have tasted death were it not for the Fall. Moreover, in being the Mother of the Creator, Mary was raised to an incomparably higher state than Eve, thereby increasing the extent of her prerogatives.

This parallelism may seem fanciful in an age when Genesis has been rendered 'mythological' by the exponents of unfettered form criticism and by post-Darwinian evolutionary theories, but to the Fathers such an approach would have destroyed the spiritual and hidden meaning of the texts which, after all, is the way in which Christ himself understood the Scriptures. Hence St Irenaeus writing as early as 177 AD, explains why Mary can in truth be called the Second Eve:

---

[16] Justin Martyr *Dialogue with Trypho*. Quoted in Palmer SJ p 12

"For as Eve was seduced by the word of an angel to avoid God after she had disobeyed His Word, so Mary, by the word of an angel, and the glad tidings delivered to her that she might bear God, obeying His Word. And when the former had disobeyed God, yet the latter was persuaded to obey God in order that the Virgin Mary may be the advocate of the Virgin Eve. And as the human race was sentenced to death by means of a virgin, it was set aright by means of a virgin."[17]

The crucial importance of the second Eve imagery is here made explicit by St Irenaeus when Mary and Eve are linked by virtue of their salvific significance. Eve's disobedience which with Adam brought death is undone by Our Lady's *fiat*. This grace-filled surrender to God's will allows St Irenaeus to refer to her as both 'advocate' and, in strictly qualified sense, as co-redeemer. The human race is 'set aright' by Our Lady, not by any intrinsic merit she has by right but by virtue of her co-operation with sanctifying grace, a co-operation which is so perfect that it can be truly said to be a necessary part of man's salvation. This cannot be said of any other human being. Our co-operation with grace also makes us 'co-redeemers' of ourselves, but the nature of our co-operation does not have the universal significance which Our Lady's had. If this comes as a shock to anyone unfamiliar with the Fathers' mariology, it must always be set within the context of their Christology. Hence St Irenaeus' eulogising about Mary is as nothing when compared to his sublime theology of 'recapitulation' through which he expresses his understanding of Christ's divinity. If Our Lady is the second Eve, her divine Son he describes as the second Adam, but an Adam who confers divinity on his creatures. Hence for St Irenaeus He is the 'perfect Bread of the Father ... the

---

[17] St Irenaeus *Against Heresies* quoted in Palmer SJ p 13

Bread of Immortality.'

Our Lady's mediation which is a reflection of the great mystery of grace and free will, is perfectly captured by St Irenaeus when he writes:

> "For while the sin of the first man was emended by the correction of the first born,
> the guile of the serpent was overcome by the simplicity of the dove (Mary)."[18]

In another passage Our Lady's power over the serpent is ascribed to her power of intercession:

> "It was right that Eve should be summed up in Mary, That a Virgin should be a virgin's intercessor, and by a Virgin's obedience undo and put away the disobedience of a virgin... And the trespass which came by the tree was undone by the tree of obedience, when, harkening unto God, the Son of Man was nailed to the tree ... And seeing that He is the Word of God Almighty, whose invisible presence shed in us and over the entire world, He still continues His influence in the world, in all its length, height and depth."[19]

As for all the Fathers, so with St Irenaeus. Our Lord's Incarnation is the actual medicine of immortality. He sanctifies and divinizes through His Divine Grace which has its source in Him. In this sense He is the only redeemer. But Our Lady allows the medicine to be administered by Her consent. In this sense Her co-operation is truly one of co-redemption. St Irenaeus depicts this as the dove overcoming the guile of the serpent. The dove by her humility, purity and prayerfulness, allows the serpent to be destroyed. Her immaculate virtues draw down upon Her body

---

[18]   St Irenaeus *Against Heresies* quoted in Palmer SJ p 13
[19]   Quoted by Jean Danielou SJ in *From Shadows to Reality* p 45

and soul the pre-existent Word, almost like a magnet attracting iron to itself. This is Her co-redeeming as understood by the Fathers as early as the second century.

St Peter Chrysologus who died in 450, saw in Mary's Divine Motherhood a mystical significance akin to the Mosaic role in Exodus.[20] In the eighth century St Germanus of Constantinople explicitly carries these truths, expressed hitherto in mystical language, to a level of petitionary prayer. In *sermon 9*, Our Lady is invoked as the 'unfailing hope of Christians', as the co-redemptrix ('For no-one, Lady all holy, is saved except through thee'), as the mediatrix of all graces ('No-one, Lady most vulnerable, is given the merciful gift of grace except through thee'), and as refuge of sinners.[21] Although these formal invocations are a development of the earlier Fathers, making explicit that which was already present in embryonic form; an excellent example of Newman's theory of development, but applied to the Church's worship.

From this and other writings, it is evident that so exalted a position do the Fathers give Our Lady, her honour and glory give rise to a role analogous with that of Her Divine Son. As a creature redeemed by the infinite merits of Her Son, she is part of His Mystical Body as are all the baptised. As the second Eve, Her co-operation with the Redeemer gives her an intercessory and expiatory power which is, with the correct qualification, analogous to Her Son who redeemed Her. This, of course, assumes that the Fathers shared a theology of the Communion of Saints which included intercession by the saints in heaven and sanctification as the indwelling of Christ in the soul.

In this way, the references by the Fathers to Our Lady's power to save can become understandable. It is a power derived from Her Son, through Her maternal mediation. This mediation

---

[20] St Peter Chrysologus Sermon 146 *On the Generation of Christ* quoted in Palmer SJ p 39

[21] St Germanus of Constantinople Sermon 9 quoted in Palmer SJ p 57

first and foremost arises from Her intercessory prayer for Her Son's children. The use of the word 'mediation' in this context, implies no more than the obvious fact that all Christians when praying for one another, are acting as mediators. This is a derived mediation and qualitatively and essentially different from the proprietary mediation of Christ, the God-Man. The Fathers certainly understood this. It is clearly not possible to examine all the texts indicating this but the writings of St Ephrem give the clearest possible indication of patristic mariology, being both typical and early in composition. His orthodoxy and his sanctity are not disputed in the East or the West. It is difficult to understand how Newman could have read his devotional works and not become convinced of the continuity between Roman devotion and that of the fourth century Eastern Church.

In his hymns to the Blessed Virgin Mary, St Ephrem gives clear expression to a mediatorial role of the Virgin Mary. This he does by stressing Her intercessory power. The following passage portrays Her as interceding for the fallen Eve, by way of intimate conversation with Her Son:

> "Let Eve, our first mother, now hear and come to me. Let her lift up her head that was bent low under the garden's shame.
> Let her uncover her face and give thee thanks, because thou hast taken away her confusion. Let her hear the voice of perfect peace, because her daughter has paid her debt." [22]

Nowhere do the Fathers deny the fact that Our Lady had given to Her the power of intercession. This power only became contentious at the time of the Reformation, after Luther confused the theology of justification. He viewed the Catholic insistence on invocation and the associated doctrine of merit as an intrusion on

---

[22] Quoted in Palmer SJ p 19

Christ's all-sufficient mediation. The root cause of Luther's dissent lay in his inability to believe in grace as indwelling and sanctifying. In this manner he overthrew completely the Fathers' understanding of the spiritual life as divinisation. That is to say, the literal God-like qualities of Mary's Immaculate Conception, being similarly imparted to each soul through sanctifying grace. It is this which leads to the view of Newman that the indwelling Christ imparts Christ's merits and virtues to the soul. This sanctification and justification, whilst inextricably linked, are to be distinguished in the Catholic scheme.

This tradition runs from St Irenaeus to St Cyril of Alexandria in the East and is developed by St Augustine, St Anselm, and St Thomas Aquinas in the West. It is important to understand this principle, because from it the Catholic theology of merit accrues and is in turn the reason why Our Lady has been regarded with such veneration by the Fathers.

Divinisation is best conceptualised by the phrase 'God made Himself man, that man might become God.' At its most fundamental level it means an ineffable descent by the Creator to the ultimate limit of our fallen condition. Such a descent even unto death, makes possible the re-opening of the gates of Heaven by creating a path of ascent which leads to the union of created beings with the Divinity itself. Before St Athanasius, Origen seems the first mystical writer to have written in some detail on the concept. However, it is St Gregory of Nyssa who best illustrates this principle.

Unlike St Athanasius, his experience of God was a deeper and deeper embracing of darkness, so that his mystical writing is dominated by the soul's natural inability to know God, who is its insatiable longing. But it is in the darkness that divinisation takes place, for in it God is present to the soul and the soul is united with Him. Purification is central to that union, to enable the soul to contemplate God by contemplating the Divine image present within itself. St Gregory emphasises more the kenotic aspect of divinisation thus reflecting his Christology, wherein the manhood of Christ is deified by the *Logos*, being transformed into the pure, divine nature. Divinisation means that the soul's purification which is marred by sin, can reflect the Divine image. But this is not a reflection of something external to the soul: the indwelling Christ is present:

> "It is impossible for the Living Word to be present - I mean the pure invisible spouse who unites the soul to Himself by sanctity and incorruptibility - unless by the mortification of our bodies on earth we tear away the veil of flesh, and in this way open the door to the Word that He may come and dwell in the soul."[23]

With this understanding of a soul's sanctification as a very participation in the Divinity and Humanity of Christ, a sharing in His nature, it followed for the Fathers that Our Lady represented this participation to the ultimate extent. She who was privileged to contain Christ within her very womb, must have participated in His nature more intimately that any other human being. This intimateness was a direct result of her own virtues; unsurpassed virtues of supernatural faith, hope and charity, which drew down upon her, as it were, the Divine Logos. Thus her sanctity was seen by the Fathers as the pinnacle of a process of divinisation which allowed degrees and which allowed merit.

The mystical writings of St Gregory of Nyssa allow us to see how Our Lady could thus be viewed. Although no specific mention is made of her in the following extracts, there can be no doubt that St Gregory is alluding to Our Lady's virtues, inasmuch as she is the second Eve, and therefore a representative figure. In common with St Gregory Nazianzus, St Gregory of Nyssa had no

---

[23] Commentary on the Song of Songs XII 1016c

qualms about the title 'Mother of God', nor about defending Our Lady's perpetual virginity. In his treatise *On Virginity* , it is Our Lady who seems to be referred to as the embodiment of the spiritual qualities of this virtue. J N D Kelly has observed that in this work, St Gregory goes further than his contemporaries in maintaining that it was through Our Lady and her virginity that the long reign of death was undone.[24]

In his *Commentary on the Song of Songs*, St Gregory gives an allegorical interpretation in which, in keeping with the tradition, the soul's union with the bridegroom is portrayed as the lover pursuing the beloved. Later this came to be interpreted as Christ's love for His Mother as well as Christ's love for his Church. The titles given to the sections anticipate some of the titles later given to Our Lady. 'Lily of the Valley' is still used in hymns to The Blessed Virgin Mary , but other titles seem to point to Her, albeit indirectly. 'The Heavenly Tabernacle', 'The Fruit of the Apple Tree', 'The Mirror of the Church', 'An Odour of Sweetness', 'The Garden Enclosed', 'One is my Dove'. As in his *Life of Moses* so here in the Commentary, the fundamental theme is the inhabitation of the Trinity within the soul. This inhabiting of the soul is the basis of divinisation. At times it involves an ecstatic union which St Gregory variously describes; sometimes he describes it as:

> "removing the coverings of the flesh, those garments
> of skin (Gen 3:21), by putting on the wisdom of the
> flesh..."[25]

Essentially this refers to penance and mortification, undoing the damage done to our first parents. He also refers to it in more

---

[24] J N D Kelly *Early Christian Doctrines* p 495
[25] St Gregory of Nyssa *On Virginity* quoted in *From Glory to Glory* p 117

mystical terms:

> "The lily usually shoots straight up from the root like a reed, developing a flower at the top; and there is a good distance between the flower and the ground, for the reason, I think, that its beauty might remain pure up above and not be defiled by contact with the earth."[26]

Similarly, *The Fountain Sealed Up* employs mystical imagery to portray the spiritual life in terms of a supernatural growth requiring purification.[27]

Finally, *One is my Dove (p14 of MS)* illustrates perfectly the patristic allegorical exegesis. Canticle 6:8 makes reference to 'my dove my perfect one: she is the only one of her mother, the chosen one of her who bore her.' St Gregory writes of this passage:

> "Surely we know who the mother of the dove is, since we know the tree by its fruits. When we consider man, we cannot doubt that he is born of man. Similarly, if we look for the mother of the chosen dove, we will recognise her in none other than that Dove we spoke of."

This Dove, who is mother of the 'chosen dove' (Jesus Christ) is, for St Gregory, the Holy Spirit. Later writers would interpret this passage in a purely mariological sense, and seemingly less convoluted in the genders used. However, the relevant factor for us, is not the precise details of how the different Fathers rendered their interpretation, but the general method - highly mystical and allegorical. It was this, which enabled them to support their doctrinal teaching unashamedly from Sacred Scripture, and it was this which caught Newman's mind and heart.

---

[26] Commentary on the Canticle quoted in *From Glory to Glory* p 173
[27] ibid p 229

The relevance for Newman's mariology is this: the Fathers gave to Newman a dogmatically-based spirituality. He deemed such a nexus quite compatible with Anglicanism when applied to all the Christian doctrines with the single exception of mariology. This is an apparent inconsistency which can be partially explained by the Protestant nature of the Anglican formulae. What cannot be explained, however, is why the single factor of Our Lady's intercession remained so conspicuously unaccounted for in his treatment of the Fathers' spirituality. The very mysticism which we have just been examining, with its related scriptural exegesis, accounts for the mariology of the Fathers. Newman never felt able to embrace this till he had put down his pen upon the completion of the *Development of Doctrine* in 1845. Perhaps a good example of religious prejudice lying deeper we imagine.

This apparent inconsistency will be examined more closely in the next chapter. To what extent Newman embraced a Catholic devotion to Our Lady whilst still an Anglican, can be determined by his understanding of the Communion of Saints.

Chapter Two

VIA MEDIA
THEOLOGY

Upon the death of R H Froude in February 1836, it fell to Newman to choose one book as a memento from Froude's library; he chose the Roman Breviary. This was certainly a surprising choice, given Newman's antipathy towards liturgical deviation from the Prayer Book. It can perhaps be explained by the fact that having seen Froude use it as a purely private devotion, no disloyalty to the Reformation could be construed. However, as P B Nockles has observed in his thesis on the Oxford movement[28], the Tractarian quest for a thoroughgoing Catholic system with a full-blooded ideal of Catholic sanctity, led to dissatisfaction with the reformers.[29] The Old High Churchmen saw the spirituality of Antiquity and the reformers as broadly synonymous. The use of the Breviary and the subscriptions to the Martyrs memorial were the visible catalysts which highlighted a growing split among the Tractarians themselves. By 1838 Newman was openly critical of the reformers.[30] Hence his comment to Thomas Henderson:

---

[28] Published as *The Oxford Movement in Context; Anglican High Churchmanship, 1760-1857,* C.U.P., 1994.
[29] Letter to Miss Bristowe, 15 April 1866.
[30] See *British Critic* XXX1 (April 1842) p 388.
Also see letter to Henry James Coleridge, 20 October 1865, where Newman admits that he regards the Reformers as 'shufflers' i.e. disingenuous. Hence Tract 90 became feasible. Pusey thought them fully catholic.

"Cranmer will not stand examination... The English Church will yet be ashamed of conduct like his."[31]

Nockles has also made it clear that the Tractarian disillusionment with the Reformation was a spiritual one before it became doctrinal. Froude based his criteria for use of the Breviary not on antiquarian conformity but on:

" 'excellence of beauty', so that 'whatever is good and true in those devotions will be claimed.' "

With this criteria accepted, the path was open for a more obvious romanising party within the movement most forcefully represented by W G Ward and Oakley respectively. However, their more Italianate devotions did not appeal to Newman before 1841. There is a definite evidence, however, that after Tract 90 Newman advocated a restrained Tridentine spirituality, but not 'popular popery'. The latter referred to devotion to the Virgin Mary and the Saints as represented in the devotional manuals, and similar popular devotion to the Blessed Sacrament reserved. This would account for the tone of a letter to J H Bloxam in February 1841, in which Newman is challenging Catholics to emulate the pastoral virtues of their saints, and, by implication, not just a misplaced invocation:

"if the Romanists really want to convert England, let them go barefooted into our manufacturing towns, let them preach to the people, like St. Francis Xavier did, let them be pelted and trampled on, and I will own that they can do what we cannot; I will confess that they are our better far."[32]

---

[31] Letter to John Henderson March 1838. Olland MS. Pusey House. Similarly his hostility to Bishop Jewel's spirituality.
Oratory MS. Box 65, Letter to J Keble   27 August 1837.

[32] Letter to J H Bloxam February 1841 Oratory Ms. Ms. 3

If in 1841 Newman was still vehement about the Catholic doctrine of the Communion of Saints, in 1838 he was equally vehement about the Reformation liturgical changes. He regarded the reformers as men:

> "intended to Luteranise our devotions, I mean to bring in confessions of sin, unworthiness, anti-self-righteousness, justification by faith only etc, and that these very portions... do...throw the Church into a lower and sadder state of devotions."[33]

Newman was clearly in a quandary at this time. Being both dissatisfied with the reformation liturgical and doctrinal comprehensiveness, the *lex orandi, lex credendi* principle had become dislocated. His doctrinal appeal was beyond the Reformation of the Fathers, but what of his liturgical appeal? In public worship it had to be unquestionably loyal to the Prayer Book unadulterated; anything less would have provoked denunciation if not popular riots, as the ritualist controversy later showed. This is not to accuse Newman of disingenuousness; he was on the horns of a dilemma. Rome and her liturgy still contained grave abuses, notably transubstantiation and invocation of the Saints, especially the Blessed Virgin Mary. The patristic liturgy was out of the question. So long as the Prayer Book was capable of a reasonably catholic interpretation, with catholic interpreted to mean a *Via Media* theology, the Tractarian theology and Tractarian spirituality could be held together by the Prayer Book. There still remains the question of why Newman was not able to see the shaky nature of this edifice, when he had partly repudiated in 1838 both the liturgical and theological effects of the Reformation as represented in the Prayer Book. Tract 90

---

[33] Letter to J Williams 13 December 1838 Williams deposit. Lambeth Dep. 3/26

relied on a deliberate concession to an ambiguous view of both the Anglican liturgy and the doctrinal formulae. Even the Royal Supremacy came in for a rebuke in his article in the *British Critic* for October 1839 on liturgical ceremonial:

> "Let the visible be a type of the invisible. You have dispensed with the clerk, you are spared the royal arms ..."[34]

The complete answer must, by its nature, be beyond the scope of speculation and enquiry: suffice it to say, that it was his devotion to The Blessed Virgin Mary which both prevented him from becoming a Catholic, and which helped sustain him after he chose so to do. Fr Placid Murray is surely correct when, in his introduction to Newman's Oratory Papers for 15 June 1846, he notes in Newman's introductory address to the new Oratory:

> "We can detect here a mixture of Newman's heritage of Anglican devotion to the Blessed Trinity and to Our Lady as the 'Seat of Wisdom', combined with overtones of the current Catholic devotion to the Holy Family."[35]

Although the Catholic devotion to The Blessed Virgin Mary as 'the destroyer of heresies' is not quite parallel to her title as 'Seat of Wisdom', Newman's connections with institutions under her patronage may seem almost providential - Oriel College, the University Church with its south porch dominated by a Bernini style Madonna and Child, Old Oscott renamed Maryvale, and the Birmingham Oratory itself dedicated to the Immaculate Conception. Then there are his personal acquaintants - Maria Giberne, his closest female friend; Pusey, who instigated the *'Eirenicon'* exchange with its attack on certain Marian prerogatives;

---

[34]   *British Critic* XXVI p 324
[35]   Placid Murray op.cit. p 149

and most important of all, his sister Mary, of whom he was most fond. Before examining his Marian devotion, we should note the tendency in some recent Catholic writers to exaggerate this devotion whilst he was still an Anglican.

Fr Dessain's appraisal of Newman's Anglican writings as a "classical, a truly catholic Catholicism",[36] is based upon the assumption that "unlike the Roman theologians, he was brought up under the dominance of no dominant philosophy or tradition of theology. " It is true Newman knew little or nothing of the medieval schoolmen, nor of St. Thomas, but this is not to say that Newman lacked a systematic theology, nor that it somehow gave him a freer access to a golden age of pure Catholicism. Newman's theological method was really trail blazing, in that he had few precedents upon which to draw. If the Fathers were the foundation and the High Church 17th century Anglican Divines the mediators, Newman had himself alone as the criterion by which to synthesise these two components. In a number of fundamental areas this left Newman unable to produce a Catholic systematic structure upon which to build a renewed and re-catholicised Church of England. Nowhere is this more apparent than in his own understanding of the doctrine of the Communion of Saints. Fr Dessain has inaccurately maintained that Newman believed in invocation as part of 19th century Anglicans' devotions to the saints. In fact, their invocation was anathema and for Newman, was so, right up until his reception. Article XXII denouncing the invocation of saints as 'a fond thing vainly invented', was loyally adhered to, even by the community of Littlemore amidst the otherwise full recital of the Breviary offices. Fr Dessain's desire to portray Newman's theology and spirituality as a model for a Vatican II renewal, leads him to overlook aspects of Newman's writings which are incompatible with Catholicism.

---

[36] S Dessain op.cit. p 17

It is true that 'the last thing he wanted was to be thought 'a creative mind' or to be inventing some new theory.[37] But as we shall find with his Anglican Marian devotion, to hail the Blessed Virgin Mary as the second Eve after the Fathers and yet to reject her intercession, can hardly allow Fr Dessain to justify a claim that 'He had no particular doctrine of his own.'[38] This must be so in the light of Newman's later Catholic writings, where the intercession of the *Deipara*, as her refers to her, forms the very kernel of his writings. As he noted in 1865:

> "As then these ideas of her (Mary's) sanctity and dignity gradually penetrated the mind of Christendom, so did that of her intercessory power follow close upon them."[39]

The Sermon, *The Communion of Saints*, preached in the University Church on 14 May 1837, sets out what may be called loosely, a '*Via Media* Spirituality'. It was delivered in the context of the Lectures of the Prophetical Office begun in 1834 in the Adam de Brome Chapel, and published in 1837. As with the lectures, so with the sermon, Newman attempts to reconcile a Catholic view of the Church as both visible and invisible with an Anglican view of the Church as *essentially* invisible. The spiritual ramifications of this produce both a high view of the Church and a low view of the actual relationship between the church militant and the church triumphant. No mention is made of a church expectant, and only a shadowy description is given of the church in Heaven.

The Sermon opens with a reference to Pentecost and the role of the Holy Spirit in forming the Apostles into a visible society,

---

[37] ibid p 19
[38] ibid p 19
[39] *Difficulties of Anglicans* Vol II p 73 (Christian Classics edition)

with a unity derived from their being grafted into the Body of Christ. The unity, however, is *essentially* invisible:

> "the Church then, properly considered, is that great company of the elect, which has been separated by God's free grace, and His Holy Spirit working in due season, from this sinful world, regenerated, and vouchsafed perseverance unto life eternal... He dwells in the hearts of His Saints, in that temple of living stones, on earth and in heaven ..."[40]

The unity of the Church derives not from any visible structure, not even from an episcopate, but:

> "Its being alive is what makes it one; were it dead, it would consist of as many parts as it has members; but the living *Spirit* of God came down upon it at Pentecost, and made it *one*, by giving it *life*."[41]

Newman realises that this is not compatible with a patristic understanding, so he next introduces the role of the episcopate:

> "When we approach the Ministry which He has ordained, we approach the steps of His throne. When we approach the Bishops, who are the centres of that ministry, what have we before us but the twelve Apostles, present but invisible ?"[42]

Prior to this, the three branch theory is used by Newman to try and resolve the dilemma between an essentially invisible church known only to God, and the manifestation of that church visibly on earth. Thus on the one hand the church:

---

[40] P P S IV:II (1868 edition) pp 172-173
[41] ibid p 171
[42] ibid p 177

"is not locally or visibly on earth. The church is not in time or place, but in the region of spirits."[43]

and on the other:

"the bodily presence of Bishop and people, are given to us as keys and spells, by which we bring ourselves into the great company of the saints; they are as much as this, but they are no more; they are not identical with that company."[44]

Herein lies the key to Newman's understanding of the Communion of Saints. The three so-called episcopal communions (Greek, Roman and English) have a privileged access to the Heavenly Jerusalem. They form the 'visible porch' which, after baptism, gives a soul on earth company with 'the one invisible company of elect souls.' In emphasising that the Church is brought to perfection in Heaven, and that the vast majority of the church is to be found in Heaven, Newman confuses ecclesiology and the communion of saints.

The Via Media theology of the imperfectly realised visible church on earth represented by three episcopal communions all in schism from one another and with none recognising one another's claims - a schism within a schism - forces Newman to place the unity of the Church essentially in Heaven:

"Baptism admits, not into a mere visible society, varying with the country in which it is administered, Roman here, and Greek there, and English there, but *through* the English *or* the Greek, *or* the Roman Porch into the one invisible company of elect souls, which is independent of time and place, and

---

[43] ibid p 175
[44] ibid p 176

untinctured with the imperfections of error of the visible porch by which entrance is made ..."[45]

The effect of this ecclesiology is to render incidental, at least in theory, the visible structures of the Church. Although he placed episcopacy as the Christian ministry, as the outward visible guide of what was unseen, the reluctance of the Anglican Bishops to see themselves as the successors of the Apostles, the negative view of the Reformation, and most important of all, the increasing disillusionment with the Via Media as a viable alternative to Rome, makes Newman's description of the Church Militant and the Church Triumphant somewhat altruistic. Because the three 'Porches' are in schism from one another and at doctrinal loggerheads over fundamental issues, the relationship between the perfectly united Church in Heaven and its fractured counterpart on earth, is difficult to define. This amorphous unity on earth renders magisterial infallibility quite impossible, and can at best lead to an ill-defined 'indefectibility'. Whether this imprecise relationship between church on earth and church triumphant in Heaven accrues after schism or is also a characteristic of the Undivided Church, Newman never fully makes clear. What he does make clear in his Anglican writings on the Communion of Saints and on ecclesiology, is that the vitiated state of communion between the 'Porches' on earth impeded the communion between the church truly and perfectly Catholic in Heaven. The following passages illustrate this well. The Church Catholic is a nebulous body not really on this earth except in an amorphous, spiritualised sense:

> "And now we may form a clearer notion than is commonly taken of the Church Catholic which is in all lands. Properly it is not on earth, except so far as

---

heaven can be said to be on earth, or as the dead are still with us."[46]

It is not surprising that with such a highly mystical view of the Church Militant, Newman should interpret St Cyprian's maxim 'extra ecclesiam nulla salus', as referring to 'that great invisible company, who are one and all incorporate in the one mystical body of Christ . . . This *invisible* body, is the *true* Church, because it changes not, though it is ever increasing."[47]

The ramifications of such a synthetic ecclesiology are felt in Newman's devotions to the saints. He defines the doctrine of the Communion of Saints as:

> "the nature and attributes of this Church, as manifested in the elect, as invisible, one, living and spiritual."[48]

The same, essentially invisible nature of the communion, is reflected in *Verses on Various Occasions*. Where specific mention is made of the intercession of the saints, it is always a reference to a saint alive, praying for a church militant, never to a communion between visible and invisible.[49] This understanding is in stark contrast to his Catholic writings, in which Newman invariably presents a majestic, yet intimate, familial unity between the Church Militant and the Church Suffering and Triumphant. Within this context, 'communion' means intercession. Intercession is the means by which communion is expressed and manifested. The closest Newman is able to come to an

---

[46] ibid p 175

[47] ibid pp 174-175

[48] ibid p 171

[49] See Verse CXVI *Intercession of the Saints*, where the 'saint' referred to is Moses on Mount Sinai praying for the Israelites, and Verse XCVI *The Church in Prayer*, where Peter is referred to as a saint whose main task is preaching not praying - 'a truant in untimely rest'.

intercessory communion as an Anglican, is expressed in the following:

> "When we are called to battle for the Lord, what are we who are seen, but mere outposts, the advanced guard of a mighty host, ourselves few in number and despicable, but bold beyond our numbers, because supported by chariots of fire and horses of fire round about the mountain of the Lord of Hosts under which we stand."[50]

Newman does insist that this prayer is an essential role of the church triumphant, but he is unequivocal in condemning the invoking of such prayer:

> "And further, it must be considered that though the Church is represented in Scripture as a channel of God's gifts to us, yet it is only as a body and sacramentally, not as an agent, nor in her members one by one."[51]

This is a curious understanding of the Church as the mediator of Divine grace, and is undoubtedly reflecting his Via Media theology where a Church Militant renders impeded the intercessory and evangelistic function of its members. Bishop Butler had noted this grave defect of the Anglo-Catholic 'three-branch theory", as being totally inconsistent with any pre-Reformation tradition:

> "The Branch theory implies a meaning for the word 'society' which is quite other than the Roman Catholic meaning of the word, and than the pre-reformation meaning..." Similarly for the Orthodox... "the visible Church essentially of its very nature, a single communion... As regards the

---

[50] P P S IV:II p 177
[51] ibid p 183

> nature of the Church, the Anglo-Catholics stand on
> the Reformed side of the great divide in Western
> Christendom."[52]

With an imprecise and defective Church Militant, the Church Triumphant assumes an intercessory power independent of the visible church on earth, so that in his Anglican sermons on both the nature of the Church and the nature of her communion, an essentially Protestant theology is unconsciously displayed. Hence in the above sermon the Church is distinguished from being an 'agent' by its being a 'body'. This is a curious distinction. Newman is virtually insisting that grace is conveyed only through the sacraments, and by way of corporate activity. The intercessory power of the saints in Heaven and most particularly Our Blessed Lady being rejected by Newman, forces him to locate the unity of the Church on earth in an unspecified sacramentality which gives rise to the 'body' imagery of St Paul, whilst the prayers and merits of the faithful on earth united with the saints in Heaven, in being rejected, does not allow Newman to view the Church, either on earth or in Heaven, as an 'agent'; i.e. as a Divinely-appointed mediator. This is fundamental. Because of its defective unity on earth it cannot only fail to realise a perfect union with the Church in Heaven, but it is incapable of mediating Divine Truths on earth. A theology of mediation in the Catholic sense means that God in His infinitely gracious Mercy condescends to make Himself dependent upon His human creatures in His workings. Paramount in this mediation is His Church - in Heaven, Purgatory and on Earth.

A stark contrast to this loosely-defined relationship, is presented by his Catholic sermons, where the visible Church on earth reflects more definitely the Church in Purgatory and in

---

[52]   Bishop Butler OSB *The Idea of the Church* pp 21 & 30

Heaven. The sermon preached at the first provincial synod of Westminster in July 1852, illustrated this ecclesial harmony in intercessory communion:

> "One thing I am sure of, that the more the enemy rages against us, so much the more will the saints in Heaven plead for us; the more fearful are the trials from the world, the more present to us will be our Mother Mary, and our good Patrons and Angel guardians; the more malicious are the devices of men against us, the louder cry of supplication will ascend from the bosom of the Church to God for us ... By the intercession of the Saints on high, by the penances and good works, and the prayers of the people of God on earth, you would be forcibly borne up as upon the waves of the mighty deep, and carried on out of yourselves by the fullness of grace, whether nature wished or no ... (and of St Philip). As he was with you three centuries ago in Rome, when our Temple fell, so now when it is rising, it is a pleasant token that he should even set out his travels to you; and that, remembering the relations he then formed with you, he should now be wishing to have a name among you, and to be loved by you, and perchance to do you a service, here in your own land."[53]

Apart from the obvious ability to identify with precision the visible Church, the intimacy with the Church Triumphant is now unmistakable. Equally unmistakable is the sheer power of intercession enjoyed by the Saints and Angels, a power which increases proportionally as does Satan's. Because Newman is now certain that the visible Church corresponds in its essence with the Roman Church, he is thereby assured that Her canonised saints

---

[53] *Sermons on Various Occasions* pp 180 & 182

correspond with the Church in Heaven. The bond is now identifiable and the communion certain and experiential. This must not be dismissed as a minor feature of his theology of the Church or of his spirituality. The effect on his prayer life is dramatic, as dramatic as the doctrine of infallibility was on his theological method. Newman's devotion to the Blessed Virgin Mary will illustrate both these points.

Chapter Three

HOW FAR TO GO ? (1825 - 1845)

Of the Catholic devotion causing most difficulty to the Anglican Newman, none was more problematic than devotion to Our Lady. In the *Apologia*, he himself confesses that upon being given a book of Marian devotions compiled by St Alphonsus de Ligouri, he had complained:

> "Such devotional manifestations in honour of Our Lady had been my great *crux* as regards Catholicism."[54]

It is ironic then, that in his *Essay on the Development of Doctrine*, Newman devotes just two short sections to Marian doctrines and devotion. The first, to illustrate the fifth test of a faithful development (Logical sequence), he uses to show the essentially Christological basis of Marian devotion, in particular, as a basis for detecting heresy:

> "The votaries of Mary do not exceed the true faith, unless the blasphemers of her Son came up to it. The Church of Rome is not idolatrous, unless Arianism is orthodoxy."[55]

The second, is used to illustrate the sixth test of authentic development, that of preservative additions. The question Newman was seeking to answer was that of the Christological basis of Marian devotion. This was no longer a problem once he had

---

[54] *Apologia* p 244
[55] *Essay on Development* p 408

digested the full implications of the Council of Ephesus'
sanctioning the title 'Mother of God'. It protected the faith of
Catholics from 'a specious humanitarianism', and thus he could
write:

> "if we take a survey of Europe at least, we shall find
> that those religious communions which are
> characterised by the observance of St. Mary are not
> the Churches which have ceased to adore her
> Eternal Son, but such as renounced that
> observance."[56]

The problem tackled in this short section is that of the
popular Catholic Marian devotions. Newman concludes that they
do not constitue an impediment to the worship of her Divine Son.
His approach is an interesting one. By assessing the timbre and the
atmosphere of the prayers directed towards Our Lord and to Our
Lady respectively, rather than a strict liguistic analysis, he can
conclude:

> "How different, for instance, is the tone of the *Dies
> Irae* from that of the *Stabat Mater* . . . how distinct
> is the language of the Breviary services on the
> Festival of Pentecost, or of the Holy Trinity, from
> the language of the services for the Assumption!
> How indescribably majestic, solemn and soothing is
> the *Veni Creator Spiritus*. . . How gentle, on the
> contrary, how full of sympathy and affection, how
> stirring and animating, in the Office for the
> Assumption, is the *Virgo prudentissima, quo
> progrederis, quasi aurora valde rutilans?* . . . It would

---

[56] ibid p 434 The 1878 revision makes the point more clearly:
" ... we shall find that it is not those religious communions which are
characterised by devotions to the Blessed Virgin that have ceased to
adore her Eternal Son, but those bodies ... which have renounced
devotion to her."

seem then that whatever be the influence of the
doctrines connected with St. Mary and the Saints in
the Catholic Church, at least they don't impede or
obscure the freest exercise and the fullest
manifestation of the devotional feelings towards
God and Christ."[57]

These words were written after Newman had resolved to
become a Catholic. It would seem that the Marian devotion of
the Catholic Church, itself, fell naturally into place in Newman's
mind, in much the same way as transubstantiation had done.
Once the realisation dawned, that Rome was where the fullness of
Christ's teaching authority lay, then the problematic dogmas were
resolved by antecedent probability and his theory of doctrinal
development.

It is a remarkable fact, however, that given the Anglican
objection to the invocation of the saints, and more particularly to
the rejection to the doctrine of the Immaculate Conception,
explicitly in article XV, and implicitly in article IX of the thirty-
nine Articles of Religion, Newman had such an intense love of the
Mother of God. This is first revealed, surprisingly, in an
unpublished sermon delivered on the Feast of the Annunciation
1831. Of his 126 *St Clement's Sermons*, none is preached directly
on Our Lady, Newman's prime concern in these being to preach
the evangelical doctrine of the atonement. We should note here
Newman's reading under Walter Mayer's influence, and later the
influence of Sumner's book *Aposotolical Preaching* and Milner's
Church History. In his *Journal*, Newman reveals that the last author
had kindled in him great love for the patristic period as early as
1825, even though he did not read through the Fathers
systematically until the summer vacation of 1828. These writings

---

[57]   ibid, pp. 436, 37 and 38.

with their profound awareness of Christ's divinity and incarnation, must have sown the seeds for a great respect for the Blessed Virgin Mary. However, as early as 1825 Newman is referring to Our Lady as the 'Mother of God', which is remarkable, given the evangelical fear of mariolatry. In a sermon preached on 'Religious Joy', Mary is high-lighted as the illustrator of the workings of Divine grace. The Incarnation, as the supreme example of divine condensation, is the means by which men become partakers of Christ's divinity:

> "Men we remain, but not mere men, but gifted with a measure of all those perfections which Christ has in fullness, partaking each in his own degree of His Divine nature so fully, that the only reason (so to speak) why His saints are not really like Him, is that it is impossible - that He is the Creator, and they His creatures; yet still so, that they are all but Divine, all that they can be made without violating the incommunicable majesty of the Most High."[58]

This sermon must surely reflect strongly the influence of Milner's *Church History*. It is doubtful whether Keble or Milner enjoyed an intimacy with Newman at this stage; Pusey was still suspect, and Keble's influence was most strongly felt in 1827 with the publication of *The Christian Year*. Hence, all the more remarkable is the Patristic idea of divinisation so obviously reflected, and the implication that the Virgin Mary was the highest of all the saints:

> "in proportion to the mystery is the grace and mercy of it; and as is the grace, so is the greatness of the fruit of it."[59]

Mary is referred to as being higher than every other creature:

---

[58] P P S VIII:17 p 253 *Religious Joy* preached on Christmas Day 1825
[59] ibid p 252

'higher than the Angels or Archangels, cherubim or seraphim', on account of divinising grace, a destiny open indeed to all men. There is no evidence to suggest that Newman had become formally disillusioned with evangelicalism at this stage. He was still wrestling with the baptismal regeneration issue at this time. Pusey accused him in February of the next year of becoming more High Church, and soon after he was to sever formal links with the Bible society. It must be assumed then, that Newman's respect for the Mother of God, was for him, a logical corollary from his belief in the Incarnation. This approach remained acceptable to his fellow Anglicans, so long as the thirty-nine Articles were not breached by invocation or any hint of co-mediation. This then accounts for the fact that Newman's Marian sermons produced no outcry.

To understand fully Newman's devotion, it must be remembered that the context of his sermons was either the University Sermons of the day, or more particularly Morning Prayer from Cranmer's *Book of Common Prayer*. Newman was preaching to the generation prior to the illegal additions and alterations made by the High Church clergy, who later became known as ritualists. This group, reflecting the dissatisfaction with the Protestant nature of the Anglican liturgy which only began to surface in the next decade, carried that dissatisfaction one step further than say Froude and his disciples. They actually interpolated ceremonial, and later ritual, into Cranmer's Communion Service directly culled from the *Missale Romanum*, and which had been deliberately expunged by the reformers. However, it was not until the following generation again, that public devotion to Our Lady dare be incorporated into the Anglican liturgy, and then, only by a tiny 'extreme' minority. To this day the official Anglican liturgy allows no invocation of the saints, even though the calendar has been extended. Of the twenty-one saints days observed in the Book of Common Prayer, the Blessed Virgin Mary had two red letter days with collects, and one without (the Conception), with which Newman would have been familiar. Neither of the two feasts allocated collects (the Presentation in the Temple, and the Annunciation) makes any reference to Our Lady herself.[60] This is in marked contrast to Newman's later devotion, wherein the liturgy observed forty-one Marian feasts with prayers of invocation, and where there were five direct invocations of her in the invariable liturgy. The net result of Cranmer's reforms, was effectively to allow popular devotion to the Blessed Virgin Mary to fall into oblivion, the Caroline divines notwithstanding. This is the *lex orandi, lex credendi* lying behind Newman's sermons at this time. They are clearly remarkable in the light of this.

In his first published sermon dealing with the reverence due to the Blessed Virgin, Newman is at once exalted in his portrayal of her and cautious in the reverence he gives to her. Her unfathomable virtues and purity are meditated upon, paramount amongst which is her apparent sinlesssness:

> "What, think you, was the sanctified state of that human nature, of which God formed his sinless Son; knowing as we do, 'that which is born of the flesh is flesh', and that 'none can bring a clean thing out of an unclean ?' ... but there are those who go in a calm and unswerving course, learning day by day to love Him who has redeemed them, and overcome the sin of their nature by His heavenly grace ... And, of these undefiled followers of the Lamb, the Blessed Mary is the chief."[61]

Although this is only a veiled reference to her Immaculate Conception, and understandably so, it is one of the chief features

---

[60] It is true that Cranmer retained the Magnificat at Evensong, but to what effect ?

[61] P P S II:12 *Reverence due to Her* pp 132 & 136 (25 March 1832)

of Newman's Marian devotion, both Anglican and Catholic that she who gave her flesh in order to incarnate the Word, must of herself have been conceived without sin. in the *Meditations and Devotions*, Newman devotes seven meditations to the Immaculate Conception alone, and most of his correspondence about Mariology as a Catholic was about this dogma. This sermon, preached as it was in 1832 after he had finished reading the Fathers for the first time, reflects the patristic understanding of Our Lady as the second Eve. After Christ himself as the New Adam, Our Lady is the second Eve, upon whom the process of recapitulation itself depends. Hence Newman, in adopting the patristic theme, uses imagery traditionally adopted in Catholic devotion to depict the Immaculate Conception:[62]

> "In her (Mary) the destinies of the world were reversed, and the serpent's head bruised ... in her the curse pronounced on Eve was changed to a blessing."[63]

We have observed that in describing Our Lady as the 'second eve' and 'undefiled', Newman is only *hinting* at the Immaculate Conception. This has to be stressed; indeed, when set alongside a later sermon, it would seem he was never able to realise fully what he had been implying. A sermon delivered in March 1837, *The Mystery of Godliness*, explicitly denies the possibility of her being conceived without original sin:

> "No one is born into the world without sin; or can rid himself of the sin of his birth except by a second birth through the Spirit."[64]

---

[62]   Cf. The Apparitions to St Catherine Labouré, 1830, and ensuing devotion

[63]   P P S Op.cit pp 128 & 129

[64]   P P S V:7 p 90

It is interesting to note, however, that in this sermon he uses the same text as in the earlier sermon to argue for mankind's sinful nature, which before he used to illustrate Our Lady's Immaculate Conception - 'Who can bring a clean thing out of an unclean ?' Clearly, by 1837, Newman would have been fully acquainted with the Catholic dogma. By 1832, however, his reading may not have encompassed this, particularly when we remember that in the following year he was still quite unfamiliar with the Catholic cultus of the Blessed Sacrament. To the question, 'what must have been the transcendent purity of her, whom the creator Spirit condescended to overshadow with His miraculous presence?", Newman is afraid to answer, curtailing his meditation with the words:

> "this contemplation runs to a higher subject, did we dare follow it ... Had Blessed Mary been more fully disclosed to us in the heavenly beauty and the sweetness of the spirit within her, true *she* would have been clearly seen; but, at the same time, the Giver would have been somewhat less contemplated, because no design or work of His would have been disclosed in her history."[65]

Newman hints at what may be the 'higher subject'. It is the co-mediation of Mary in our redemption:

> "the more we consider who St Mary was, the more dangerous will such knowledge of her appear to be. Other saints are but influenced or inspired by Christ, and made partakers of Him mystically. But as to St Mary, Christ derived His manhood from her, and so had an especial unity of nature with her; and this wondrous relationship between God and man it is perhaps impossible for us to dwell much upon without some perversion of feeling."

---

[65] P P S II:12 p 134

And further,

> "... And when sorrow came upon her afterwards, it
> was but the blessed participation of her Son's sacred
> sorrow, not the sorrow of those who suffer for their
> sins."[66]

The perversion of feeling referred to, is the exultation of
Mary which impedes the all-sufficient mediation of her Divine
Son. Given the Protestant theology of grace and merit enshrined
in the Prayer Book, such a passage is, nevertheless, truly
remarkable. The reference to the sorrows of Our Lady, carries
with it a veiled reference to her sinlessness as well as an equally
veiled reference to her co-mediation resulting from her proximity
to that Divine suffering of her Son. He clearly states that Our
Lady's suffering is qualitatively different from that of sinners
which is partly punitive; hers by contrast is participatory, and that
in an unique way. We see in this sermon the embryonic devotion
to Our Lady which is such a notable feature of Newman's
Catholic writings; here indeed, is a genuine continuity between the
Newman of Oriel College and the Newman of Birmingham
Oratory. It is also a splendid illustration of the *lex orandi, lex
credendi* principle.

The prohibition on invocation enshrined in the Anglican
Articles of Religion, Newman loyally respected. Such a practice
was said to impede the all-sufficient mediation of Christ, a fact
Newman clearly concurred with, seemingly unaware of the same
problem arising if one allowed the saints to pray for the faithful,
without their actually being invoked.[67] The rejection of a theology

---

[66]   ibid pp 135 & 137

[67]   Cf.   the implication throughout the sermon 'The Communion of
Saints' that the Church triumphant is guarding and praying for the Church
militant: e.g. "shall we doubt for a moment, though St Paul was martyred

of lesser mediation, through prayer and penance, by Cranmer led to this suspicious attitude towards the cult of the saints - a clear example of doctrinal and devotional interdependence.

More subtle, however, is the reason why Newman is wary of Our Lady's co-mediation. It is not just a question of invocation, but a more fundamental misunderstanding of grace and merit. Ordinary saints, he asserts, do not obscure the worship the God's grace in them, because they can be 'seen working *towards* an end appointed by God, we *see* him to be an instrument.' With Our Blessed Lady it is different; first, the nature of her vocation is so sublime, so intimate and so incomprehensible, that 'it is a dangerous thing, it is too high a privilege, for sinners like ourselves, ... we cannot bear to see such men (women) in their own place, in the retirement of private life, and the calmness of hope and joy.'[68] This is not a question of invocation impeding the all sufficiency of Christ's sacrifice, but the sheer overwhelming sanctity of the individual. Such a degree of sanctity, Newman maintains, because of its awesome degree, and private nature, threatens to keep our devotional attention focused on her, a creature, rather than God the originator of such grace and sanctity. It is for this reason Newman concludes, 'that so little is revealed about the Blessed Virgin Mary, in mercy to our weakness.' For this reason, too, he extols the Prayer Book observances of Our Lady's feasts as being equally festivals of Our Lord:

> "for nothing is so calculated to impress on our minds that Christ is really partaker of our nature, and in all respects man, save sin only, as to associate Him with the thought of her, by whose ministration He became our brother."[69]

---

centuries upon centuries since ... the Mountains of the Saints ?"
P P S , IV:II pp 179-180
[68] *P P S,* II:12 p 134
[69] ibid p 136

Newman's objection to anything more than a restrained devotion, based on a veiled and imprecise knowledge of her sanctity, appears to have been anticipated in Apostolic times. Medieval theologians frequently ascribed to St Denys the Areopagite, a sentiment whereby anyone who saw Our Lady in the Apostolic days after the Ascension, would have mistaken her for a goddess, such was her beauty. Hence the Apostolic silence about her prerogatives. Such also is the view of St Louis Marie de Montfort who as a Doctor of the Church seems to have uncritically assimilated this tradition.[70] This reticence certainly seems more understandable in pre-Nicean devotion, but is less easily so, when the Divinity of Christ is no longer questioned, at least in a manner calculated to jeopardise Mary's creatureliness. It is almost as if Newman secretly acknowledges to himself the implications of Mary's Divine maternity - i.e. that it necessarily involves both an intimacy with her Creator and a derived holiness, which demands a role for her more than Cranmer has given her. This he dare not concede consciously, let alone publicly. Consequently, we find in this sermon, the paradoxical attitude of Newman, which finds him putting Mary on a pedestal greater indeed than any Italianate devotion, and yet denying her the veneration the faithful have traditionally found to be the basis of her intercessory power as the humble 'handmaid of the Lord'.

The second reason Newman adduces for being wary of devotion to Mary, is that ordinary sinners find her very presence

---

[70] St Louis Marie de Montfort (1673-1716). A French missionary priest who laid the foundation for union with 'Christ Wisdom' as essentially through Mary, in his major work the *True Devotion*. His theology is anti-Jansenist in tone. The true devotion, refers to Our Lady as the Mother of Divine Grace and hence Mediatrix of all Graces, with all her clients' merits, prayers and good works being consecrated to her. Pius XII canonised him on 20 July 1947.

overpowering; she is 'too calm, too joyful', etc. This calmness and joy are said too obscure the grace of God, so that the instrumentality of her soul is impossible, or at best, difficult to see. The instrumentality of a created soul, refers to its being an instrument by which ultimate union is achieved by the grace and mediation of *Christ* - because of any intrinsic qualities meritorious in themselves. Again, this objection is difficult to understand when one considers Newman's understanding of the patristic principle of divinisation. The unsurpassable sanctity of the Blessed Virgin Mary should have been seen simply as the clearest possible exemplar of the power of sanctifying grace at work in an ordinary, humble, Jewish maiden. It is true that the fact of the scourge of original sin in other mortals distorts her 'ordinariness'. Clearly Newman is handicapped here by an imprecise theology of her Immaculate Conception and of mediation.

Newman's inability at this stage, to give a full veneration to Mary without fearing an obscuring of Christ's Divinity, arises from the Protestant nature of the Anglican formularies. The Catholic theology of merit, whereby man's acts performed in a state of grace contribute towards his justification, was officially repudiated by Cranmer, and incorporated into Article XI of the thirty-nine Articles. Similarly, Article XIV led to the curtailing of pious acts of devotion, which again were believed to carry merit. On a more fundamental level still, it is the very workings of Divine grace which produced this fundamental divergence. The Catholic understanding viewed grace as both a gift and a character, which, when co-operated with, perfected nature and enabled the recipient to acquire merit - a mysterious interdependence, with the absolute priority of God preserved by the doctrine of pre-venient grace. Newman, by the time this sermon was preached in 1832, was well on the way to embracing such a view; for example, his sacramental development over baptismal regeneration, and his reading of the mystical theology of the Fathers, with their view of sanctifying grace as a divinisation. However, without a theology of merit, he could only regard the saints as exemplars of Divine grace rather than participators, though the mystical body, in a special way in the atoning work of Christ. Although Newman's teaching on the indwelling Christ went a long way to reconcile the Anglican and Catholic view on justification, the Catholic insistence that grace can be increased by good works, and that the person in the state of sanctifying grace really merits a supernatural reward from God,[71] allows a Catholic to view Mary's sanctity and her mediation as pointing to Christ. Sanctifying grace effects an inner equivalence between good works and the eternal reward. St Thomas Aquinas explains it thus:

> "Since our action has the character of merit, only on the presupposition of the Divine ordination, it does not follow that God is made our debtor simply, but His own, inasmuch as it is right that His will should be carried out."[72]

In this way the devotion paid to the saint, whether it be veneration of him or invocation of him, can be a mediatorial devotion without detracting from the hypostatic mediation of the

---

[71] See *Denzinger* 779 Decree of the Council of Trent

[72] *Summa Theologica* Q 114 Article I 'Whether a Man can Merit Anything from God ?'
Gerald Manley Hopkins in his poem *The Blessed Virgin Mary compared to the Air we breathe* makes the same point with reference to Mary's intercessory power:
'She holds in high motherhood
Towards all our ghostly good ...
More makes, when all is done,
Both God's and Mary's Son ...
Through her we may see him
Made sweeter, not made dim,
And her hand leave his light
Sifted to suit our sight.'

Son. Without this perspective, Newman could only view Our Lady's sanctity as giving rise to a false mediation, if penetrated too deeply. Hence his extraordinary warning not to look at Our Lady's hidden and inner life too closely; 'the higher their gifts, the less fitted they are for being seen.'[73] Such an attitude to the saints contrasts markedly with traditional Catholic piety where they are seen by many writers on the spiritual life as fulfilling Our Lord's exhortation to put our lamp on a lampstand.[74] Newman's approach is a sort of doctrine of reserve without knowing what the doctrine is !

The result of this attitude to grace and merit is, that when Newman does attempt to write about Our Lady, it is in ethereal and ineffably poetic tones:

> "But in regarding Mary, we look to one whose actions we know not of and cannot, if we would, too closely imitate, whose name recalls to us bright and pleasant thoughts, the emblem of early devotedness to God, guiltless piety, angelic purity, meekness, modesty and patience, shining only in the light of her Son and in the effable radiance of that Spirit of power who came upon her and overshadowed her, and hence receiving the prize of that high salutation of Gabriel: 'hail, thou art highly favoured (filled with divine gifts), the Lord is with thee, blessed art thou among women.'[75]

As with the use of the formal title 'St Mary', he is here writing *about* her, never addressing her. This is the single most

---

[73] P P S op cit p 134

[74] Cf. The Decree *Lumen Gentium* no 50 of the Second Vatican Council, where devotion to the Saints is clearly set in the theology of the Mystical Body. As such, they draw us on to Heaven, *away* from ourselves and onto Christ.

[75] *Mariologie* 139 Quoted in *The Mystery of the Church* p 93

obvious distinction between his Anglican exemplar theology, with its lofty almost unapproachable attitude, and his Catholic devotion which seems more intimate, and paradoxically, less exalted.

Soon after this sermon was preached, Newman did compose a verse whilst on his Mediterranean tour, which comes close to an invoking of Our Lady to protect him from 'the Tempter's dart':

"Thou, who didst once thy life from Mary's breast
Renew from day to day,
Oh, might her smile, severely sweet, but rest –
on this frail clay !
Till I am thine with my whole soul; and fear,
not feel a secret joy, that Hell is near.'[76]

It is true there is no direct request to Our Lady for her help, but the implication is that she gave Our Lord sustenance in his manhood, so she can similarly strengthen the weakened humanity of sinful man. Her 'severely sweet' smile, implies a gentleness in her intercession, which is, at the same time, uncompromising in its desire for perfection in the supplicator. How far Newman was conscious of this maternal role in the economy of redemption, is impossible to say. Like so much of Newman's Tractarian writings, more is hinted at than Newman himself seems aware of, hence the confusion and storm over Tract 90 and Charles Kingsley's accusations arising out of *Wisdom and Innocence*. Newman himself admitted that it is often better to understate a case and let the reader wrestle out the true meaning. It is salutary to remember that Newman's love for the Fathers was firstly a love for their mystical approach to their theological method. We can note the influence of Butler as giving to Newman, as did Keble, the regard for dogma as conveying a sacred truth enshrined in rites and

---

[76] *Verses on Various Occasions* p 127   Verse LXXII
'Temptation' composed on 28 March 1833 at Frascati.

ceremonies. G D Rowell has argued that this sacramentalism culled from the Fathers, is the major basis for Newman as an ecumenical figure:

> "When Pusey wrote that Newman had been so formed in Anglicanism and had been translated to the soil of Rome, the nature of the formation to which he referred was primarily a scriptural and patristic one ... The debt owed to the Greek Fathers in the formation of his theology gives him an ecumenical significance in dialogue with the Orthodox Churches."[77]

The great problem for Newman in writing about Our Lady as an Anglican was the clear disjunction between patristic witness to her as an intercessor, which was a doctrine to be found primarily in the Eastern liturgies, a doctrine which went hand in hand with her role as *theotokos*, and Anglican liturgy, which clearly rejected the former, and yet, which appeared to uphold the latter. If, as Dr Rowell insists is the case, Newman perceived Christian theology as sacramental and liturgical because it is first and foremost incarnational,[78] then the mysticism he discovered in say StÊAthanasius or StÊJohn Chrysostom, had to be compatible with a Prayer Book whose entire ethos was reformed in character. This is reflected in a sermon on the Incarnation preached on Christmas Day, 1834.

Newman here gives a classic exposition of the Catholic doctrine of the Incarnation, relying heavily on St Athanasius. There is a striking allegorical description of Our Lady 'as a garden inclosed, a spring shut up, a fountain sealed.'[79], which really most effectively illustrates Newman's Marian piety. The intrinsic

---

[77] *Ecumenism* in Gweten-Theologie-Leergezag pp 52 & 53
[78] ibid p 50
[79] P P S II:3 p 32

qualities and virtues which Newman readily ascribes to Our Lady, are not for public devotion or scrutiny; they are solely for the purpose of incarnating the Eternal Word, lest she intrude upon the Divine mediation of her Son. Even the title 'Mother of God' is now only used tentatively, (cf. 'she, if it might be said, the Mother of God', p2) and her sinfulness definitely asserted, despite a previous passage arguing for the virgin birth on the basis of Our Lord's sinless humanity. In another sermon, Newman actually maintains that the believer's union with Our Lord is more intimate than that of His Mother's.[80] There is a timidity about this passage which is perhaps reflected in the fact that it is only one out of three references Newman makes in public to the Blessed Virgin Mary after the substantial sermon of 1832. There is, it is true, a verse dedicated to St Joseph written in January 1833, whose content seems more fitting when applied to the Blessed Virgin Mary, so intimate and ambiguous are the sentiments,[81] and also Verse LXXII, referring to Mary's mediation, to which we have already referred. These apart, there is only one other reference to Mary until after his conversion.[82]

What is there to account for this silence, given the exalted tones of the Candlemas sermon of 1832 ? The answer must lie in the Anglican liturgy. With the rare recital of the Nicene Creed, due to the scarcity of any eucharistic celebration, and the equally

---

[80]   P P S IV:16   *Christ Hidden from the World*   p 247
[81]   'O Purest Symbol of the Eternal Son !
       Who dwelt in thee, as in some sacred shrine
       To draw hearts after thee, and make them thine;'
       Verses on Various Occasions Verse LXIV p 118
[82]   In the sermon *The Theory of Developments in Religious Doctrine*, University Sermon XIV
       (2 February 1843), Newman views 'St Mary' as 'Our Pattern of Faith'.

rare recital of the Athanasian creed, the Anglican liturgy only provided for the most meagre reference to Mary - i.e. in the Apostles Creed and The Magnificat. Cranmer had expunged all reference to her from the collects (cf. the collect for Christmas Day, it being a notable exception) and from the Communion Service with the exception of Christmas Day. Certainly the anthems of Our Lady recited after Vespers or Compline were not permitted, these forming the most important invocations of the Virgin in the pre-reformation liturgy. We have made mention of this already as being incompatible with the patristic sacramental mysticism of the Fathers. If this be true, it must be asked, what would Newman have read from 1828 onwards concerning Our Lady which would have been incompatible with the Anglican liturgy ? It is impossible to answer this question with certainty. But it was systematic reading he began in that year, and as such, reference to the liturgy would have been made, certainly in the sermons of St John Chysostom, the writings of St Basil of Caesarea and St Cyril of Alexandria. The Nestorian heresy in particular would have impressed upon Newman the upsurge of devotion to the Virgin in response to the attack on her title *theotokos*. From this period quickly evolved two of the earliest Marian feasts - the Dormition or Assumption of the Blessed Virgin Mary, observed before the year 500, and the Nativity of Our Lady. Even if Newman was not familiar with the Byzantine liturgical tradition from his initial reading of the Fathers, the Mediterranean tour of 1833 certainly revealed to him the ethos of the Patristic liturgy, for it inspired sentiments of devotion to the Mother of God, not to be forthcoming again, until after his conversion, including direct invocation.[83] Upon his return to England, it would not be for another six years before he would deviate from the official Protestant liturgy, and then only in

---

[83] Cf., Verse C *Hora Novissima* op cit, with its reference to 'my Mother' and 'her sacred shrine'.

private and with scrupulous care not to infringe Cranmer's mariology.

Hilda Graef, in her comprehensive study of mariology, has shown that as early as 230, Our Lady's prayers were being invoked. St Gregory of Nyssa makes reference to the vision of St Gregory the Wonderworker who died in that year in which Our Lady is hailed as able to save. Similarly, a direct prayer is addressed to her in an early 4th century manuscript: 'Mother Of God hear my supplication: suffer us not (to be) in adversity, but deliver us from danger'.[84] A text Newman must have come across as an Anglican, is Gregory Nazianzus' *Oratio* XXIV, 11 (2). Here there is an unequivocal evidence for the cult of Our Lady as intercessor, for St Gregory refers to a virgin imploring Her help.[85] This confirms what we observed in Chapter One.

The only conclusion to be drawn is that Newman placed loyalty to the thirty-nine Articles higher than the devotional pattern of the Fathers. In this respect he was following the tradition of the Anglican reformers who had declared the Eastern Orthodox Churches to have erred, 'not only in their living and manner of Ceremonies, but also in matters of Faith.' (Article XIX) Such articles of religion are no longer said to be authoritative by some Anglicans, and by others, only in a general sense; but in Newman's day it was not so. In the University they were rigorously applied both as tests for under-graduate and graduate members, and to contravene their strictly Protestant interpretation could result in deprivation of degree and living. Tract 90 and W G Ward verify this. They could be by-passed to a certain extent on eucharistic doctrine, due largely to a greater degree of ambiguity in other parts of the Prayer Book, but Marian devotion was different. The empty niches were vivid reminders of the

---

[84] H Graef *Mary, a History of Doctrine and Devotion* pp 47 & 48
[85] ibid p 64

previous idolatry, the restoration of which, only the next generation dare attempt, but in a manner of which Newman disapproved.[86]

[86] *Anglican Difficulties* Vol 1 p 224 (Uniform edition) 'It is pleasant to adopt a habit or a vestment; ... But it is like feeding on flowers, unless you have that objective vision in your faith, and that satisfaction in your reason, ... they cannot be made to rest on the influence of individuals. ... If your externals surpass what is within, you are, so far, as hollow as your evangelical opponents'. Similarly, *A Letter to Henry Wilberforce* 24 December 1848 in which Newman expresses his disdain for 'Puseyism': 'He is not reviving anything that *ever* was *any* where for 1,800 years.'

Chapter Four

THE CATHOLIC MEDIATRIX (1845-1890)

If it be accurate to assert that the Protestant nature of Anglican liturgy inhibited Newman's natural high regard for the office of the Blessed Virgin Mary from becoming the 'Virgo Veneranda', then we would expect to find a twofold effect upon his reception into the Catholic Church. First, the catholic features of his Anglican spirituality will be brought over, but in their new *sitz im leben* a transfiguration will be noticed deriving (a) from the presence of an infallible magisterium, and (b) from a liturgy more readily enshrining that spirituality. Secondly, new doctrines and devotions will be embraced which hitherto were found unacceptable. Newman's devotion to the Blessed Virgin Mary encapsulates the process well, and as such, is deemed a fitting example of his Catholic spirituality as a whole.

Newman's love for Our Blessed Lady cannot be questioned in the light of his Anglican writings. If as an Anglican there is only one published sermon explicitly devoted to her, his Catholic sermons reveal a burgeoning. In his *Meditations and Devotions* there are thirty five devotions and meditations about her. In the *Sermon Notes* there are fourteen sermons preached about her and frequent references to her in the 165 other notes. Discourses XVII and XVIII in *Discourses to Mixed Congregations*, and are explicitly about her, whilst the most famous sermon Preached on Various Occasions[87], in its central section is addressed to her. Important also are the verses written after 1845 in *Verses on Various Occasions*,

---

[87] "The Second Spring", p.177.

number four in honour of Our Lady, not to mention the role given to her in *Dream of Gerontius*.

The Letters and Diaries contain references to Our Lady, usually in the context of correspondence with non-Catholics who have difficulty in understanding the Marian prerogatives, most notably the Immaculate Conception. It was not, however, this medium which Newman chose to express his Marian devotion. He naturally took for granted the Church's dogmatic teaching about her, and even if he preferred the more restrained English manuals _ and there is some doubt about this as will be seen _ there can be no questioning his complete and utter obedience to the magisterium. This was challenged by Mr Kingsley in his attack upon the integrity of Catholic priests, and it evinced the following reply from Newman:

> "Let me take a doctrine which Protestants consider our greatest difficulty, that of the Immaculate Conception ... I have no difficulty in receiving it. ... So far from the definition in 1854 being a tyrannical infliction on the Catholic world, it was received everywhere on its promulgation with the greatest enthusiasm. ... My simple question is whether the assumption of infallibility by the proper authority is adapted to make me a hypocrite."[88]

This passage tends to confirm what we have already noted; that after 1845 the *lex orandi lex credendi* principle becomes properly integrated in a manner not possible before this. As with his eucharistic devotion so with his Marian; this infallible magisterium allows the creation of a total certainty in truths that hitherto were tentatively evinced by the Via Media ecclesiology, or else unacceptable altogether. Newman is now able to believe in

---

[88] *Apologia* pp 288 & 296

Our Lady's Immaculate Conception, not because he has made some startling new discovery whilst working on the *Development of Doctrine*, nor because he surrendered the integrity of his intellect to an infallible teaching authority, but because no other Church conforms as closely to the teaching of the Fathers as does the Catholic, and therefore, it must be the 'pillar and ground of all truth'. The spiritual benefits of this realisation for Newman, are reflected in his Marian devotions. It must be stressed once again that the doctrinal basis for Newman's conversion cannot be divorced from the spiritual. Catholic doctrine and devotion are inextricably linked, so his objection to the so called extreme Italianate devotions which bedevilled him right up to his submission, dissolved, once he realised they did not obscure Christ's mediation. This realisation may or may not have preceded his conversion, or rather may have been coterminous with it and demonstrated once again the inter-dependence of doctrine and spirituality. It is impossible to know which came first - acceptance of Our Lady's Catholic prerogatives, or belief in her intercession and co-mediation. The *Essay on the Development of Doctrine* implies a dogmatic acceptance of *theotokos* as pointing to Our Lady's intercession, preceding his acceptance of the later devotions, but this is by no means certain from the context, which is illustrating the fifth and sixth tests respectively of true development.[89] What is certain, is that as little as three years after his conversion he had reversed even his reluctance to use what he calls 'foreign books of devotion'.

---

[89] Cf. Chapter 7, p 434 where her title of Theotokos gives rise to language which is 'affectionate and ardent, as towards a mere child of Adam' and later, Newman is amazed at the restrained tones of devotion in forty little manuals of devotion from Italy, which he obtained whilst writing the *Essay*. These proved crucial in his accepting the Catholic theology.

A sermon preached in St Chad's Cathedral in 1848, because of its comparative proximity to his Anglican days, illustrates the radical change that had taken place. Newman by this time, had been ordained less than a year and had just seen to the inauguration of the Oratory at Maryvale. He had chosen the feast of Purification for this, thereby preserving a link with Oriel whose foundation day also occurred upon this feast. More particularly, Newman had chosen this Marian feast so that the new Oratory might be 'under the shadow of *Maria Purificans*'. This sermon contains a reference which throws into doubt the popular view of Newman's spirituality that it was essentially 'restrained' by comparison with continental forms. It must be remembered that he and his fellow converts had spent just over twelve months at the Collegio di Propaganda, where their spiritual diet would have consisted of all that was extant in Rome at the time. The Letters and Diaries reveal glowing accounts of the Roman baroque churches, a style Newman much preferred to Gothic, and more importantly, glowing accounts of the liturgy therein, particularly at the Chiesa Nuova, which was to become Newman's mother Church. Then, as today, this Church was noted for its liturgical excellence which was anything but restrained, reflecting the wishes of St Philip Neri for a glorious and spectacular liturgy. If Newman had desired an austere liturgy the Oratory was not the place to find it, a fact amply testified to in the present day Oratory at Birmingham. Hence it is not surprising to find Newman exhorting such devotions in this sermons:

> "I do not wish you to take up books containing the praises of the Ever Blessed Virgin, and to use them and imitate them rashly without consideration. But be sure of this, that if you cannot enter into the warmth of foreign books of devotion, it is a deficiency in you. To use strong words will not mend the matter; it is a fault within which can only gradually be overcome, but it is a deficiency, for

this reason if for no other. Depend upon it, the way to enter into the sufferings of the Son is to enter into the sufferings of the mother. ... Let her be your great pattern."[90]

At the time of preaching this sermon Newman had been surrounded by a batch of enthusiastic converts from St Wilfred's Cheadle. These 'Wilfridians', as Faber christened them, undoubtedly encouraged Newman to adopt foreign as well as English devotional manuals, but it is untrue to say that these devotions were essentially foreign to the spirit of Newman, as Wilfred Ward implies.[91] The row over *The Lives of the Saints* which, under Newman's auspices, were to be published by the Oratory Fathers, clearly reveals that Newman had no scruples about such devotions. It is true that some seventeen years later, in his published letter to Dr Pusey replying to his *Eirenicon*, Newman did concede the wisdom of not publishing such lives on the grounds 'of the effect of Italian compositions, as unsuited to this country'.[92] But in the same letter Newman also indicates that what he learnt and used in Rome he did not consider to be 'Italianate'. To what this appellation refers is not entirely clear. If *The Lives of the Saints* he later considered 'Italianate', perhaps it is an uncritical fervour which is characterised by this term. To be sure, it is not a question of any doctrinal objections, as Newman's letter to Pusey makes quite clear:

> "I prefer English habits of belief and devotion to foreign from the same causes, as by the same right, which justifies foreigners in preferring their own.. In following those of my people, I show less singularity, and create less disturbance than if I made a flourish with what is novel and exotic. And

---

[90] *Catholic Sermons of Cardinal Newman* p 103 'Our Lady in the Gospel'

[91] W Ward op. cit Volume I p 204

[92] Quoted in W Ward op. cit Volume I p 214

> in this line of conduct I am but availing myself of
> the teaching which I fell in with on becoming a
> Catholic; and it is a pleasure to me to think that
> what I hold now, and would transmit after me if I
> could, is only what I received then."[93]

That which he received on becoming a Catholic, was not simply the old Catholic piety, but devotion to St Philip Neri, St Francis de Sales, and, above all, the full Marian devotions to be found in the Raccolta, which Ward himself admits Newman was deeply devoted to, including the devotion to the Immaculate Heart of Mary. This then is the context in which those features of his Anglican spirituality which either complemented or enriched the 'external objective substantive creed and worship' he found in the Catholic Church.

In examining his Anglican Marian piety, we noted features which form a genuine continuity with Catholic faith and practice. It has to be said, however, that this dogmatic area, Newman's Anglican position, whilst laying the foundations for his later piety in the Catholic Church, does not meet the *full* requirements of Catholic teaching. This has to be emphasised because of recent deviations amongst Catholic theologians who attempt to justify their position by having recourse to Newman, invariably citing his Anglican theology. Fr Dessain certainly adopted this tactic in his last years, thus emulating Tyrrell and lesser known modernists such as William J Williams. Like Fr Dessain, these writers make little or no reference to Newman's Catholic devotions, which must be the most accurate way of assessing how his theology is to be interpreted. It surely must be said that neither the neurotic Newman depicted by Bremond, nor the Newman moulded by the liberal *'periti'* of the Second Vatican Council and their present successors, is compatible with the Newman of the Raccolta or the

---

[93] Letter to Dr Pusey, quoted in W Ward Volume I op.cit p 214

devout client of Our Lady. For example, Newman's Anglican theology of the real presence is not unlike Schillebeeckx' transignification theory, representing as it does a rejection of a theology of 'change' in preference for a more subjective view.[94] Newman's Marian devotion before 1845 can likewise be compared to such radical Catholics who reject Mary's role as mediatrix of all graces or her role as co-redemptrix in the scheme of salvation. The ARCIC catechism in its 71st article represents such an approach, when it emphasises Our Lady's role as an exemplar of Christian faith, and with an understanding of the communion of saints very much in accord with the Anglican Newman.[95] It must be emphasised these views represent a continuity only in so far as the full Catholic doctrine is left unstated.

The *Meditations and Devotions* form the bulk of his Marian piety, ranging from a mediation on the Litany of Loreto, with its

---

[94] Cf. Pope Paul's Credo of the People of God where this view is decisively rejected and transubstantiation reasserted as the only acceptable philosophy to help explain the mystery.

[95] See Article 70 where the dogma of the Immaculate Conception is defined in a similar manner: 'these doctrines do not concern Mary alone: she is the archetype model of the working of God's grace in all the faithful'. (Vatican II Decree on the Church Number 63). The members of the commission have quoted Number 63 out of context. The decree makes it quite clear that the Immaculate Conception is an *unique* grace given for an unique function, and that Our Lady is 'Advocate, Helper, Benefactress, and Mediatrix.' Newman would also have been less than content with the omission of any reference to Our Lady's intercession. Cf. *Lumen Gentium* Number 69: 'The entire body of the faithful pours forth urgent supplications to the Mother of God ... also Number 67. Let them carefully refrain from whatever might by word of deed lead the separated brethren ... into error about the true doctrine of the Church.'

recitation of the traditional invocations, to devotion to the Immaculate Heart of Mary; the former has a comparatively venerable pedigree, whilst the latter required Newman to compose his own litany which he recited for the fortnight prior to the Feast of the Assumption. His litany of the Holy name of Mary was a similarly original composition and one which complemented the litany to the Immaculate Heart, being recited during the fortnight after the Assumption. In his prefatory notice to the collection, Fr Neville revealed that it was Newman's custom to mediate with pen in hand, and to note down those thoughts he considered to be significant, with a view to amplifying them later. The prayers contained therein, Newman himself regarded as important, and can be said to represent a genuine insight into his spirituality. It is surprising to find that neither Fr Stephen Dessain nor Fr Placid Murray make anything more than a fleeting reference to this work.[96] Fr Strange in his work *Newman and the Gospel of Christ*, in his important section on the Indwelling Christ, make no reference whatsoever to his Catholic writings on the subject, and in particular to Newman's *Meditations on Christian Doctrine* III, where the spiritual ramifications of such a concept are expressed.[97] Even where a Catholic edition of Volume IV of the *Parochial and Plain Sermons* is referred to, Fr Strange implies that alterations were forced upon Newman, in particular, a reference in the

---

[96] See C S Dessain op.cit. p 97, where the only reference is to St Philip's devotion to the Holy Spirit, but in a wider context to 'deification' and St Athanasius. Fr Murray refers to the *Meditations and Devotions* thrice. None of these refers to Newman's love of Our Lady, and is merely repeating a point.

[97] *Meditations and Devotions* p 442 'God and the Soul'. See also *Letters and Diaries* XXVIII, Letter to John Douglas Sandford 21 November 1876; and *Discourses to Mixed Congregations** pp 188-189, all of which display a theology of grace which expands upon Fr Strange's expostion. (*Available from the publishers of the present volume.)

Anglican version to Christ being closer to the believer than His presence to Our Lady.[98] It was not a question of toning down Newman's original teaching but of magnifying it, to give to Our Lady an unique indwelling by her Divine Son. It is true, as Fr Dessain noted, 'the Fathers praised Our Lady because '*prius concepit mente quam corpore*[99], but so perfect was her act of faith which preceded the conception in her womb, that alone would have given her an intimacy with her Son beyond any other creature.[100] This is what Newman was safeguarding in the Catholic edition of Volume Four, not a reluctant mariology. The fact that the 1868 edition reverted to the original text, is no sign of a preference for his Anglican theology; it was a corporate edition and contained a number of references incompatible with Newman's known views at the time.

The neglect of Newman's Marian devotion by scholars is to be regretted. It provides a concentrated illustration of the Dogmatic Principle allied to a fervent piety, and perhaps more than any other doctrinal area, shows how the two are necessarily married. The neglect of this area of Newman's writings is understandable. Newman especially is now a laudable ecumenical reconciler. So much of his Tractarian writings are fully compatible with the teachings of the Catholic Church as Newman himself acknowledged.[101] Accordingly, writers have tended to concentrate

---

[98]   To substantiate this interpretation Fr Strange cites Fr Dessain's reference to the Fathers maintaining that Our Lady conceived Jesus in her heart before she conceived Him in her womb. As a Catholic, Newman never doubted this. (See *Catholic Sermons of Cardinal Newman* p 97).

[99]   Quoted in R Strange *Newman and the Gospel of Christ* p 153

[100] See St Thomas Aquinas, *Catena Aurea* Volume 3 (St Austin Press) p 29, where St Ambrose makes this same point.

[101] Cf. *Difficulties* Volume 1 (4th edition) p 72, where he reminisces with the utmost fondness about the Communion service in St Mary's.

on these, and that which is peculiar is overlooked. G D Rowell writing from a high Anglican perspective has concentrated on Newman's patristic heritage as the single most significant factor in Newman as an ecumenical writer:

> "Newman did not learn his theology from the scholastics or the divines of the counter-reformation."[102]

This, Dr Rowell concludes, 'gives him an ecumenical significance in dialogue with the Orthodox Churches ... like the Orthodox, Anglicans have not been a confessional Church whose appeal has been to the forms of common prayer as the matrix of theology.' If this be true, then Newman's prayers are crucial for the ecumenical significance, and in this respect the role of Mary as *theotokos*, and what this precisely entails, makes Dr Rowell's omission of any reference to Newman's Marian beliefs puzzling. For high church Anglicans this should form a point of unity. The question remains of how far Newman's views are compatible with what Dr Rowell calls, 'a church which has interpreted catholicity as a proper comprehensiveness', the criteria for which he defines as 'the lived experience of the worshipping community conscious of its continuity with the past and particularly with the primitive church.'

It is significant that in his *Memorandum* on the Immaculate Conception, written for Robert Wilberforce, Newman makes reference to his Anglican sermon for the Feast of the Annunciation, 1832.[103] It has already been noted that Newman

---

Also *Letters and Diaries* XXVII p 284, where the Church of England is described as 'on the side of God...' Also in the same year he wrote: 'there is a great Divine work going on in the Anglican Church', - to prepare Anglicans for the Catholic Church.

[102] G D Rowell op.cit p 53

[103] *P P S* II:12 p 127

hinted at the Immaculate Conception in the sermon and here he now acknowledges that fact. We have also seen that such a belief was not sustained. As then, so in this memoranda, Newman bases his belief on Our Lady's purity on the Fathers' regard for her as the second Eve, simply working out the logical implications of such an analogy. Eve's dependence on God's grace was none the less for her untainted condition; to be without original sin does not give either Eve or Our Lady a *nature* different from others. He also cites St Augustine as an authority:

> "Though, as St Austin says, we do not like to name her in the same breath with mention of sin, yet, certainly, she *would* have been a frail being, like Eve, *without* the grace of God ... There is no difference in kind between her and us, though an inconceivable difference of *degree* ... Thus, sincerely speaking, I really do not see *what* the difficulty is.'[104]

His Anglican rejection of this doctrine was as much out of fear of its consequences in implying a mediating role, as of it elevating her beyond human nature. Now there is a further understanding of the doctrine of the Communion of Saints, and with it a theology of merit and lesser mediation through intercession. Within that theology Mary is able to take a pre-eminent role, the root of this pre-eminence being found in her Immaculate Conception:

> "If Eve was raised above human nature by that indwelling moral gift we call grace, is it rash to say that Mary had a greater grace ?"[105]

Once a theology of intercession had been accepted, an intercession which enhanced and not detracted from Christ's hypostatic mediation, then the path was clear to accept the

---

[104] *Meditations and Devotions* p 118
[105] *Difficulties* II pp 45-46 Cf. pp 48-49

Immaculate Conception as a doctrine safeguarding Mary's role as *Theotokos*. If a grace raised Eve *above* human nature, then Mary's role as God-bearer allowed grace to raise her even higher. Without original sin, "by the aid of the first grace, she might so grow in grace, that, when the Angel came and her Lord was at hand, she might be 'full of grace', prepared as far as a creature could be prepared, to receive Him into her bosom." [106] In accepting this doctrine as a Catholic, Newman was accepting an even more fundamental doctrine than intercession and mediation. As the last passage reveals, a whole theology of grace was implied.

The Indwelling Christ is one of the most significant aspects of Newman's doctrine and spirituality. Both Fr Dessain and Fr Strange have treated the subject fully. Christ's intimate union with the believing soul derived from His own inner life as God-Man. Through the Alexandrian Christology of St Athanasius, with its decisive interpretation of the Pauline title 'first-begotten', Newman was able to perceive the significance of an orthodox Christology in terms of sanctification and not just redemption. His treatment of the life of grace as a divinization is in perfect accord with the Fathers, and although novel at the time in England, was a frequent theme in spiritual writings of the counter-reformation. [107] What gives Newman's treatment of this subject

---

[106] ibid p 49

[107] Cf. Thomas à Kempis, *The Imitation of Christ* Book IV, chapter XI; St Francis de Sales and St Ignatius Loyola, both of whom embraced an exemplar spirituality, but internalised through the sacraments; St Louis Marie Grignon de Montfort in his *True Devotion to the Blessed Virgin Mary* carries the divinization principle to its logical conclusion: 'God the Son wishes to form himself, and, in a manner of speaking became incarnate every day in his members through his dear mother ... for this reason the more He (the Holy Ghost) finds Mary, his dear and inseparable spouse, in a soul, the more powerful

such importance is the context in which he treated it, rather than inherent originality. In his Anglican setting it was the doctrine which aimed at transforming a religion of manners, based on an ethical code which was semi-pelagian and biblically based, into a mystically inspired sanctification, essentially sacramental, and involving penance and mortification in the face of original sin and a redemption wrought through suffering. The contrast was both spiritual and doctrinal, and is embodied in Newman's exposition of the doctrine of the Immaculate Conception.

We have noted his ambivalence towards this doctrine before 1845. The references to divinization and the indwelling Christ, make only passing references to Our Lady, although a sermon of 1825 makes one of the most explicit, both to her and to her sanctification by Christ's indwelling, even before he had fully read the Fathers! In addition, Newman describes in the most graphic terms possible, exactly what the process of sanctification can achieve, a description which not even his Catholic sermons exceed in sheer mystic beauty:

> "Men we remain, but not mere men, but gifted with a measure of all those perfections which Christ had in fullness, partaking each in his own degree of His Divine nature so fully that the only reason (so to speak) why His saints are not really like Him, is that it is impossible _ that He is the Creator, and they His creatures; yet still so, that *they are all but divine,* [my italics] all that they can be made without violating the incommunicable majesty of the most High. Surely in proportion to His glory is His power of glorifying; so that to say through Him we shall be made *all but* gods - though it is to say, and

---

and effective He becomes in producing Jesus Christ in that soul and that soul in Jesus Christ'. Pope John Paul II made St Louis de Montfort a Doctor of the Church in 1987.

truly, that we shall be higher than every other being
in the world."[108]

For our purposes, the description Newman makes here of a
soul in a state of sanctity, leaves it unclear as to whether or not it
applies to all devout Christians, ('saints' as in Protestant parlance),
or those specially chosen vehicles of grace, or the elect in heaven.
Probably the last, in which case the last idea quoted is difficult to
understand. Either we are 'all but gods' when we reach our
Heavenly destiny, or else higher than 'every other being in .the
world' by virtue of our baptismal regeneration. Newman does not
make clear which. Had he believed in Our Lady's Immaculate
Conception then this 'realised eschatology', with its tension
between the present and future state of grace, would have been
resolved. Without this perspective, Newman's Anglican sermons
on divinisation have a theoretical air about them; it is as if theory is
correct but the practice a little more tentative. A sermon preached
in 1840 encapsulates this well:

> "He is not a Christian who merely has not cast off
> religion; but he is the true Christian, who, while he
> is a Christian outwardly, is one inwardly also; who
> lives to God; whose secret life is hid with Christ in
> God; whose heart is religious; who not only knows
> and feels that a religious life is his true happiness,
> but loves religion, wishes, tries, prays to be religious;

---

[108] *P P S* VIII:17 'Religious Joy' This divinisation theme re-occurs
throughout the later sermons, but in less exalted terms - cf. Fr
Strange op.cit pp 148-153. Also Fr Philip Boyce OCD *The
Challenge of Sanctity* p 69. Fr Boyce refers to 'the ontological
divinisation of the soul in baptismal regeneration', a curious
expression not found in Newman. Apart from this incorrect use of
the term, no mention is made of it in any other context unless the
'dynamism of grace' is equivalent.

and, as time goes on, grows more and more religious, more fit for Heaven.[109]

Reflected here is one of Newman's constantly recurring themes - that of worldly Christianity, a refusal to face up to the radical and total demands of the Gospel, a religion of manners rather than inner renewal and sanctification. Divinisation is the concept of grace which represents this radical inner transformation. Without it, man 'is preparing for himself a dreadful fall.' Symptomatic of this attitude is the dismissal of the lives of the saints as untypical and normally unattainable, or else as privileged souls whose sanctity was forthcoming due to a conducive environment. To this Newman replies:

> "Let us not miserably deceive ourselves ... St Paul conquered, as anyone of us must conquer, by 'striving', struggling, 'to enter in at the strait gate'; he 'wrought out his salvation with fear and trembling', as we must do.'[110]

There then follows an espousal of the need for even holy men to remain abased:

> "In this world, even the best of men, though they are dead to sin, and put sin to death, yet they have that dead and corrupt thing within them, though they live to God; they still have an enemy of God remaining in their hearts, though they keep it in subjection ... It is nothing but the cross of Christ, without us and within us, which changes any one of us from being (as I may say) a devil, into an Angel ... This world is a dream - you will get no good from it ... the world is your enemy ... and how

---

[109] P P S VII:13 'Love and Religion a New Nature.
[110] ibid p 186

pleasant to be done with sin! How good and joyful
to flee temptation and to resist evil! ..."[111]

This passage, too, reflects classic themes in Newman's other
sermons on the spiritual life; the need for interior crucifixion,[112]
the danger of worldliness,[113] and obedience to an *informed*
conscience.[114]

These themes are equally present in his *Discourses to Mixed
Congregations*, and other Catholic sermons. There is present,
however, a crucial difference, at once subtle and all encompassing -
an unashamed proclamation of the Blessed Virgin Mary as both

---

[111] ibid p 186, 187, 190, 191

[112] Cf. *P P S* I:24 'The Religion of the Day' with its insistence upon the
need for the 'dark side of   religion'; IV:1 'The Strictness of the
Law of Christ'; VII:8 'The Yoke of Christ' p 108; 'Religion a
Weariness to the Natural Man' p 19; 'The World Our Enemy' p 39;
'The Duty of Self Denial' p 91; 'It is taking on us a cross a cross after
His pattern, not a mere refraining from sin'; 'The Yoke of Christ' p
105: 'Let us set it down then, as a first principle in religion, that all of
us must come to Christ ... through things naturally unpleasant to us'.

[113] Cf. *P P S* VII:3 'The World Our Enemy' ; 'The World Our Enemy?
Various 'In the World but not of the World' p 279; 'But of those
who God has a love more than ordinary He watches   over them with
no ordinary jealousy; and if the world smiles on them with no
ordinary   jealousy; and if the world smiles on them, He sends them
crosses and penances so much the   more.'; *Mixed* 'Saintliness the
Standard of Christian Principle' p 90: 'Wealth is one idol of the day'
... which Newman contrasts with the Catholic saint, Cf. p 94.

[114] See *Mixed* Discourse V p 102, where Newman makes it quite clear
that conscience must be informed by the moral teaching of the
Catholic Church: 'it (the Church of England) does not engrave upon
the hearts, it does not inflict upon the conscience, the supernatural ...
it follows when it should lead'.

exemplar of the spiritual life and God's chosen creation who *mediates* it, albeit always in total dependence on her Son. This may seem a generalisation; but in all the *Discourses* concerned with holiness and supernatural growth, Newman refers to the Mother of God in these capacities. On the death bed he prays: 'let my sweet Mother, Mary, breathe on me'.[115] The definition of a saint involves: the smile of the Blessed Virgin Mary'.[116] In the Discourse on Purity and Love, she is mentioned no less than six times in an intercessory capacity, whilst Discourse III portrays her as being one of the sure signs to indicate whether or not a man is removed from the world:

> "Men of the world, my brethren, know the power of nature; they know not the power of God's grace ... they know nothing of the presence of God, the merits of Christ, the intercession of the Blessed Virgin Mary; the virtue of recurring prayers, of frequent confession, of daily masses ... We, too, like you, should be lost sinners unless Christ had had mercy on us ... unless His saints had interceded for us ... it will never repent you to have sought pardon and peace from the Catholic Church, which alone has grace, which alone has power, which alone has saints'.[117]

More explicit still, are the last two discourses on 'The Glories of Mary for the Sake of Her Son', and 'On the Fitness of the Glories of Mary'. Both of these directly regard Our Lady as the exemplar *par excellence* of the Christian virtues, and, in being so, Newman can understand her as mediatrix of all graces.

As exemplar, Newman insists that her virtues in the first instance are derivative:

---

[115] *Discourse* VI p 123
[116] *Discourse* V p 94
[117] *Discourse* V pp 60-61

> "She, as others, came into the world to do a work,
> she had a mission to fulfil; her grace and her glory
> are not for her own sake, but for her Maker's; and
> to her is committed the custody of the incarnation .
> . . every hail Mary for her continual memory, does
> but remind us that there was one who, though He
> was all blessed from all eternity, yet for the sake of
> sinners, 'did not shrink from the Virgin's womb.'"[118]

This ensures the created nature of any mediation she may enjoy as "*Deipara*" – the term Newman uses in these Discourses to describe her essential role. He goes on to maintain that "she must necessarily be more than the *Deipara*", if she is to bear witness to God as Emmanuel:

> "For consider; a defence must be strong in order to
> be a defence; a tower must be, like that Tower of
> David, built with bulwarks'; 'a thousand bucklers
> hang upon it, all the armour of valiant men.' It
> would not have sufficed, in order to bring out and
> impress on us the idea that God is man, had his
> mother been an ordinary person. A mother without
> a home in the Church, without dignity, without
> gifts, would have been, as far as the defence of the
> Incarnation goes, no mother at all. She would not
> have remained in the memory, or the imagination
> of men ... This is why she has other prerogatives
> besides, namely the gifts of personal purity and
> intercessory power, distinct from her maternity; she
> is personally endowed that she may perform her
> office well; she is exalted in herself that she may
> minister to Christ.'[119]

---

[118] ibid, p. 350.
[119] ibid p 350-351

Our Lady's prerogatives, over and above her Divine Maternity are, like all her virtues, set by Newman fairly and squarely in the context of her Son's attributes. Because these are Divine, His Mother's attributes must be as exalted as possible to enable Her to minister to Him. This is an unique insight. To serve Divinity maternally requires awesome purity - 'for this reason she has been made more glorious in her person than in her office; her purity is a higher gift than her relationship to God.' This insight is the theological and spiritual basis in Newman's understanding, for her role as mediatrix of all graces. The basis of this purity is her Immaculate Conception.

Newman obviously believed fully in this dogma, before Pius IX's dogmatic definition of 1854, and, for that matter, before the Church officially approved the apparitions at Lourdes with their reference to the said dogma. Most of Newman's dogmatic writing on the subject occurred in the wake of Pius IX's Bull *Ineffabilis Deus* which defined that 'the Blessed Virgin Mary ... was preserved free from all stain of original sin, is a doctrine revealed by God and therefore must be firmly and constantly held by all the faithful.'[120] Newman's correspondence on this matter continues after 1854. The *Letters and Diaries* reveal a fresh impetus after the publication of Pusey's *Eirenicon*, in which Anglican objections to Catholic teaching on Our Lady were put forth. Pusey's objection centered on this dogma which he believed undermined the redeeming work of Christ, most certainly in its application to the person of Our Lady. The definition also raised the question of magisterial authority and its relationship to the

---

[120] Quoted in *The Church Teaches* p 208. It was said to be an exercise of the Pope's extraordinary magisterium, fulfilling all the requirements for an 'ex cathedra' pronouncement. 'By the authority of Our Lord Jesus Christ, by the authority of the Blessed Apostles Peter and Paul, and by our Own authority, We declare, pronounce and Define ...'

Deposit of Faith.[121]

Newman himself had no trouble whatsoever with the definition, either on the Marian level or on the ecclesiological level. Before 1854 he defended this prerogative on the grounds of tradition. Pope Sixtus IV approved the feast and Pope Innocent VIII gave approval for the invocation of Our Lady under the title of the Immaculate Conception, both Popes doing this in the 15th century. The Council of Trent excluded Our Lady from the decree of original sin. The proposition that she was born with original sin was condemned by Pope St Pius V (1566-72), and Pope Paul V (1605-21) reinforced this as did Pope Gregory XV (1721-23). Pope Alexander VII (1655-67) wrote a statement anticipating exactly Pius XI's definition. Pope Clement XI (1700-21) made the feast one of precept in the Universal Church. All of this Newman was familiar with. After the definition, opposition was from Protestants who did not hold with a Catholic view of Tradition, nor with doctrinal development, and evinced from Newman the most comprehensive treatment of Our Lady's Immaculate Conception. This is contained in a letter to *Arthur Osborne Alleyne* written on *15 June 1860*.

The letter begins by delineating what Newman considers to be the fundamental difficulty. He believes it is a question of how this doctrine can be said to be united to the Apostolic Faith. Protestants are unable to see it as such because they view the doctrine as of a primary nature within the hierarchy of truth. Catholics do not place it in this category; it is derivative, and as such, a logical development from more fundamental truths, those being Our Lady as God-bearer and the doctrine of original sin and grace. The Protestant objections hinge upon a fundamental misunderstanding of the nature of Redemption. Sanctifying

---

[121] Pusey's attitude was reflected in Austin Farrer's observations about the Marian dogmas as 'an infallible fact factory going full blast', in *Infallibility in the Church. An Anglican Catholic Dialogue* p 23

grace, which has its origin and power entirely in the atoning work of Christ, is an external gift superadded to the created soul. In this way when it enters the soul it destroys original sin ipso facto. The Protestant view sees original sin as an internal evil, which can never be fully removed.[122] In turn, justification is not the elimination of sin; sin can only be forgiven. A Protestant, Newman argues, is thus incapable of conceiving of perfection. Sanctification consists entirely of faith in Christ, and with a theology of grace forbidding a 'donum superadditum' understanding, or a dimension or substance which completes or perfects man. The Immaculate Conception, then, is a concept which the Protestant theology of grace is quite unable to accommodate. If sanctification and justification are elided, at least in practice if not in theory, then the apprehension of calvary through faith is the beginning and end of a theology of grace. Grace is faith clinging to the cross.[123] The Immaculate Conception is theoretically possible for a Catholic, by contrast, because grace can obliterate all traces of sin and can perfect nature. To the Protestant this is inconceivable given his theology of grace:

> "... Protestants consider original sin to be an infection of nature, so that man's nature now is not

---

[122] Cf Barth on *Ludwig Feuerbach* p 37. 'I know of no existence other than that of sin and misery.' Or Calvin's *Institutes* III, 14, 11 'there never was an action performed by a pious man, which, if examined by the scrutinising eye of Divine Justice, would not deserve condemnation.'

[123] G C Berkouwer in his classic worth on Protestant spirituality resents this accusation: 'Faith, though not itself creative, preserves us from autonomous self-sanctification and moralism.' *Faith and Sanctification* p 93. In rejecting any theology of merit as 'self-sanctification', and grace as infused, Berkouwer is unable to distinguish between faith and sanctification, something Newman overcame as an Anglican by rejecting evangelical piety and embracing a Catholic type mysticism.

what it was before the fall. Accordingly, to be
conceived without original sin is to have a *nature*
different from that of other men ... Now I do not
deny that Catholics consider that the natural powers
of man are enfeebled by the fall; but they do not
admit any infestion of nature ... original sin,
according to them, consists in the deprivation of the
grace of God, which was a gift external and
superadded to Adam's nature ... to a Catholic ... the
entrance of grace into the soul, as a presence, ipso
facto destroys original sin; ... '

With the understanding of sin and grace, Newman argues it
is perfectly possible to interpret the scriptural phrase 'full of grace',
as meaning Our Lady possessed the fullness of grace, thereby
overcoming original sin. Hence she can be both Immaculately
Conceived and sinless, without denigrating from the redeeming
work of her Son; this so, because all grace comes through the Son
as the Eternal Word, and the grace filled conception derives all its
significance and merit in the context of the Incarnation. The
Immaculate Conception, as Newman was to write later, reveals
that God:

"began, not by giving her the gift of love, or
truthfulness, or gentleness, or devotion, though she
had them all. But He began his great work before
she was born; before she could think, speak or act,
by making her *holy*, and thereby, whilst on earth, a
citizen of Heaven ... How did Mary become the
Rosa Mystica, the choice, delicate, perfect flower of
God's spiritual creation ? It was by being born,
nurtured and sheltered in the mystical garden or
Paradise of God. ... In those blessed gardens, as
they may be called, she lived by herself, continually
visited by the dew of God's grace, and growing up a
more and more heavenly flower, until at the end of

that period she was meet for the inhabitation in her
of the Most Holy. This was the outcome of the
Immaculate Conception."[124]

The other answer Newman gave to Protestant objections,
lies in the type of doctrine which it is. There are doctrines so
intimately connected one with another, that they 'are rather parts
or aspects than distinct from them'. In this argument, concepts
and ideas are used by Newman first enunciated in his *Essay on
Development*. Hence he can argue that the Immaculate
Conception follows on from St Justin and St Irenaeus who contrast
the first Eve with the second; or from the vague description in the
early Fathers that Mary had nothing to do with sin. The denial of
the doctrine by St Bernard and St Thomas arose from the
misunderstanding of the Patristic usage.[125] In this letter, Newman
insists that the word consubstantial was similarly misunderstood
by the Council of Antioch. He cites the Koran as evidence for the
Church's belief in Our Lady's immaculateness, as Mahomet refers
to it. To illustrate this principle of primary and secondary
doctrines, Newman turns to Trinitarian theology. The Divinity of
the Son and the Holy Ghost have to be proved independently,
whilst by contrast, the *unity* of the Holy Ghost with the Father
and Son, given the last two's divinity, it follows logically and
consequently that the Holy Ghost is God also. Similarly if God is
Almighty then the argument that He is Allwise is not a substantive
and independent doctrine.

Newman's thesis is that doctrine develops and that it
develops from an initial multi-faceted mystery, the depths of
which will never be plummeted, (the 'idea' of Christianity): if this
be true, the, he argues, the Catholic belief in Our Lady's

---

[124] *Meditation and Devotions* pp 29-32 & p 40
[125] See letter to Lady Chatterton 2 October 1865. This letter is a model
of clarity, and shows how natural Newman found the doctrine.

sinlessness is no more problematic than the Holy Ghost's Divinity; both are equally problematical. Catholic belief in Mary as *Theotokos*, and as the second Eve, are first order doctrines, which by way of legitimate development can give rise to the understanding of her sinlessness through an Immaculate Conception. In this sense the dogma is a splendid illustration of Newman's theory of development in action. In this letter of 1860, reference is made to 'pairs of propositions' forming one 'idea'. This is a Catholic way of illustrating the Anglican theory in the *Essay* using the logical force of related propositions to support the one idea, rather than Bishop Butler's term *antecedent probabilities*. They both have the same effect - certitude in relation to developed or non substantive doctrine, equal to that of the original substantive idea. There is sufficient proximity one to the other to enable the faithful to assent to the infallible magisterium in these doctrines and to be confident they are one with Apostolic Deposit of Faith. If this were not the case, Newman argues, doctrinal chaos would result. Every doctrine no matter how fundamental, is still in some sense derivative in its relation to the original idea of Christianity. In a revealed religion it cannot be otherwise. The revelation is once and for all, rendering it impossible to embrace the Object of revelation other than through a derived medium. Newman puts it thus:

> "... I put to either pairs of propositions, which form
> parts of one idea respectively, and which are such,
> that to prove the one is virtually to prove the other.
> If I may not assume this, we shall never come to an
> end in the numberless points which will have to be
> proved, in order to a real reception of any one
> doctrine of the Faith."[126]

We have noted his painfully slow conversion process, as much

---

[126]   ibid

of the head as of the heart. What we observed in Newman's writings about the Immaculate Conception is the complete integration of the two. The grave problem this doctrine posed for him as an Anglican in terms of spurious additions to the Deposit of Faith, was resolved in a twofold manner. First, by his theory of Development, which enabled him to view doctrinal integrity as only requiring probable certainty, to produce absolute certainty. This, of course, is dependent upon the presence of an infallible magisterium to enable that jump to be made. Secondly, a tender love for the Virgin in his Anglican days laid the foundation for the Catholic devotion. The interdependence of these is crucial. The first opened his mind to receive the dogmatic truth, whilst the second opened his heart to see the spiritual significance of such a dogma. Nowhere is this better illustrated than in the Memorandum on the Immaculate Conception:

> "Now I wish it observed *why* I thus adduce the
> Fathers and Scripture. *Not* to *prove* the doctrine
> but to rid it of any such monstrous improbability as
> would make a person *scruple* to accept it *when* the
> Church declares it ... Consider what I have said. Is
> it, after all, *certainly* irrational ? Is it *certainly*
> idolatrous ... You may see no reason at all to believe
> the voice of the Church; you may not have attained
> to faith in it - but what on earth this doctrine has to
> do with *shaking* your faith in her, if you have faith,
> or in sending you to the right-about if you are
> beginning to think she *may* be from God, is more
> than my mind can comprehend." [127]

Newman's position is clearly summed up in the letter of 1860:

---

[127] This *Memorandum* was written by Newman for Robert Wilberforce to help him meet Anglican objections to the doctrine. See *Meditations and Devotions* p 125

> " ... the sum of what I have said is this: I fully grant that there is not that formal documentary evidence for the doctrine in question which there is for some other doctrines, but I maintain also that, from its character, it does not require it."

We have maintained that this dogma is the bedrock of Newman's Marian devotion after 1845. This is not to deny the centrality of Our Lady's Divine Maternity nor her title as *Theotokos*, but to maintain that it is the doctrine which enabled him to view her through Catholic eyes as Virgo Potens, and Cause of Salvation, both titles which Newman used in his prayers.[128] It is not without significance that there is to be seen in Newman's rooms today a small shrine to Our Lady of Lourdes which he erected soon after the apparitions of 1858. The dogmatic words of the Mother of God, 'I am the Immaculate Conception', Newman embraced with the same simplicity of faith as did the unlettered St Bernadette. This was not a problem for the Catholic Newman.

---

[128] See ibid pp 102 & 121

CONCLUSION

Vatican II in its decree *Lumen Gentium* made it quite clear that devotion to Our Lady was to continue as an intrinsic part of the Catholic Faith. The fact that the section on mariology was set within the decree on the Church does not in the least minimalise this fact. Pope Paul VI stressed this in his Apostolic Exhortation *Marialis Cultus*, and, by formally invoking Our Lady under the new title *Mater Ecclesiae*, urged the faithful to retain their devotion to Her.

Herein lies the significance of Newman's mariology for a Catholic. Coming from an Anglican background, he was forced to come to grips with a theological and spiritual idea which was intrinsically repugnant. Those extreme 'Italianate' devotions cut the ground under Rome's claim to be Apostolic. Yet the disintegration of doctrine in the Church of England undermined its claim to be Catholic. What was he to do ? The answer: to pray fervently, and study hard. The theology of the Fathers begun at the desk and then taken to the cold, austere chapel at Littlemore, lifted the veil of misunderstanding. *Theotokos* of the fourth and fifth centuries, could become the mediatrix of all graces. A genuine development was discerned and not a distortion. The effects of this discernment cannot be over emphasised. It proved the truth of the development of doctrine, and in so doing, pointed decisively to the Roman Church as Christ's One, Holy, Catholic and Apostolic Church. The development of Marian dogma and the ecclesiological development of Rome, for Newman, went hand in hand.

Catholics should never regard their Marian devotion as an obstacle to Christian unity. Newman certainly did not. He prayed for the graces of enlightenment, and in God's own time they were granted. From the moment of his reception he never once compromised or apologised for his profound love of Mary. To have done so would have been to render unnecessary the six years of unremitting soul searching which had begun with a Christological heresy and ended with mariology. What begun in 1839 as an apparent academic question of Christ's two natures, inextricably expanded, so that by 1844 Newman had come to the conclusion that Rome was the 'pillar and ground of truth' and that the Church of England was in error. In other words, if the monophysites were the catalysts, the Marian devotions of Rome were the critical 'accretions' which exploded the Via Media myth. Not for Newman a half-hearted Anglican Prayer Book red letter day. It was now, 'Our Lady, Queen of the Most Holy Rosary, *ora pro nobis*'. The shift is decisive.

For Anglicans, the fundamental break which the 1845 conversion involved, is brought home by comparing Newman's Marian devotion before and after 1845. This contrast gives lie to the view, now common, that in 1845 he was simply taking onboard a few extra Roman doctrines upon what was still essentially an Anglican vessel. This, we have shown, is not the case. Whatever else transpired between Blessed Dominic Barberi and Newman on that wet and windy night of 8 October, it was not an exchange of ideas. Newman had to abjure his former heresy and make a profession of faith based upon the decrees of the Council of Trent. The reception was more like leaping a river than crossing a bridge.

At a time when Anglican/Catholic dialogue seems destined to equivocation, and that even before the Marian dogmas have been discussed, Newman is a refreshing contrast. His letter to Dr Pusey, in reply to his *Eirenicon*, is a reminder to all those engaged in ecumenical discussion, of how truth and charity can be combined. Neither side sought compromise, both maintained their respective positions. However, Newman demonstrated the Anglican position to have misunderstood the Catholic, and most especially the dogma of the Immaculate Conception. Pusey never become a Catholic, but many Anglicans did, when Newman's tender and dogmatic love of Our Lady lifted the veil of misunderstanding. Newman realised first and foremost that devotion to Our Lady was a devotion to safeguard Her Son. His warning that that those Churches which no longer love Her, invariably no longer properly adore Her Son, gives to his Catholic mariology a crucial significance.

SELECT BIBLIOGRAPHY

Hilda Graef   *Mary, A History of Doctrine and Devotion*

J H Newman   *Apologia Pro Vita Sua*
                          Fontana Edition London 1972
                       Certain Difficulties Felt by Anglicans
                       In Catholic Teaching Volumes I & II
                          Christian Classics Westminster Md. 1969
                       An Essay on the Development of Christian
                              Doctrine (1845) Pelican 1974
                       Meditations and Devotions
                          Longmans & Co London 1893

St Louis de Montfort *The True Devotion to the Blessed Virgin Mary*
                          Montfort Publications New York 1987

Pope Paul VI   *Marialis Cultus*   Vatican Polyglot Press
                          Catholic Truth Society London 1974

Pope John-Paul II   *Redemptoris Mater (The Blessed Virgin Mary in*
                       the Life of the Pilgrim Church)
                          Catholic Truth Society London 1978

P B Nockles   *The Oxford Movement in Context:*
                          Anglican High Churchmanship 1760-1857
                              Cambridge University Press 1994

St Thomas Aquinas   *Catena Aurea* Volumes I to IV
                              The Saint Austin Press 1997